NEW PATTERNS
FOR
CATHOLIC EDUCATION

NEW LONDON, CONNECTICUT

NEW PATTERNS

FOR

CATHOLIC EDUCATION

THE BOARD MOVEMENT
IN THEORY AND PRACTICE

Daniel R. Davies

and

James R. Deneen

in association with

Russell Shaw

CROFT EDUCATIONAL SERVICES

First printing: November, 1968
Second printing: February, 1969
Third printing: February, 1970

*To the memory of
Monsignor O'Neil C. D'Amour
who devoted his last years to promoting
the board movement, convinced that it offered
the best guarantee of a continuing and effective
Catholic Church presence in education.*

Preface

This book is for those who serve on Catholic boards of education. It was written to convey to board members—present and potential—a sense of the traditions, goals, needs, and problems of the Catholic educational system; a sense of the scope and importance of the board's role; and a practical sense of how to render board service most effectively.

It is our thesis, as the reader will quickly note, that the Church has an immense and vital job to do in educating the children who look to her for their schooling. We hold that no means of carrying out that work offers so much promise as the board movement of recent years. In April of 1968, Bishop William E. McManus, superintendent of schools in the Chicago Archdiocese, declared that "elected boards, with the laity in the majority, are Catholic education's best hope for progress in the future." He so stated in his funeral sermon for his friend and colleague, Monsignor O'Neil C. D'Amour, superintendent of education in the Diocese of Marquette, Michigan; and to that epitaph for a great educator, the authors of this volume respectfully add, "Amen."

We hope that this introduction—for a single volume can be no more than an introduction to so vast and complex a subject—will whet the reader's appetite for more information.

To those readers seeking more knowledge as they master what we offer here, we recommend the readings listed at the end of this volume—and particularly the Davies-Brickell System for parish boards and the companion system for diocesan boards, which contain much more detailed suggestions on board operation.

Finally, the authors wish to acknowledge the contribution of Russell Shaw, who edited the manuscript and instilled much of its unity. They also acknowledge a debt to one another, but in the final analysis each of them takes full responsibility for the chapters he undertook to write—Daniel R. Davies for Chapters V, VI, VII, and VIII; and James R. Deneen for Chapters I, II, III, IV, and IX.

D.R.D.
J.R.D.

Contents

How Catholic Education
Is Organized

THE SCHOOL STRUCTURE

It is inaccurate to speak of the structure of the Catholic school system as though it were systematic or highly standardized. The kindest description of Catholic school administration one can offer is to say it is highly diversified; a more accurate term might be "chaotic." Some attempt will be made here to generalize about administrative functions and relationships as they were traditionally and sometimes are today found in Catholic schools; but these will truly be overgeneralizations, even as descriptions of poor practices. Catholic school administration today is clearly in transition. Any attempt to describe administrative roles during this period of change must be tentative and only moderately accurate.

Since Catholic schools grew within their Church's structure, it is not surprising to find in the schools much intermingling of ecclesiastical and educational authorities. In any line and staff drawing, the bishop of the diocese would be placed at the head of the diocesan school system as shown in Figure 1.

He assumed this position because, first, frequently all diocesan properties were titled in his name, and second, because education in Catholic schools was viewed as completely under the Church's direction and serving the Church's purposes. Catholic schools arose in this country in no small measure from the need of the Church to preserve the religious faith of its members. Since all matters of faith were within the authority of the chief pastor of the diocese, Catholic schools as extensions of the Church's teaching mission were brought under the ultimate jurisdiction of the bishop.

Traditional Catholic School System Structure

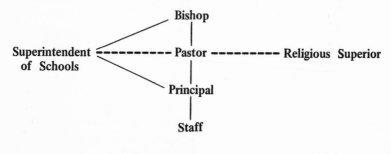

FIGURE   1

One very practical reason for maintaining the bishop's authority over the diocesan system was the atomization of that "system" into parochial fiefs. Each parish was independent of diocesan offices in staffing and financing its school. The parish manager, the pastor, could thus afford to ignore directives from all but the single person who had true preceptive authority over him, the bishop. Thus the direct line of authority in most school matters proceeded from bishop to pastor to principal. It is first at the principal's level that we meet an officer in the direct line who possesses professional educational expertise. When a parish was lucky enough to have a competent principal and a pastor who confined himself to clear, minimal, and achievable policy directions, the result was usually quite effective, if not very democratic, school administration.

Since school finances were normally in the hands of

pastors, and school budgets indistinguishable from parish budgets, expenditures were often a source of friction between school and rectory. One near-disastrous result of this arrangement was frequently seen in the method of hiring lay teachers. As nonprofessional educators and controllers of the parish purse strings, pastors frequently set very different standards for teachers than did their principals. In the absence of professionally-prepared budgets for teacher pay, salary schedules tended to hover at whatever level pastors felt compelled to pay. Since diocesan school officers usually either had no established professional standards and salary schedules, or were unable to enforce them, the deterioration of teaching staffs in parochial schools was tragically frequent during the nineteen-fifties.

As Figure 1 shows, two other functionaries appear in the traditional Catholic school structure. One is the diocesan superintendent of schools who is seen as immediately under the authority of the local bishop, with jurisdiction over school principals. Since the diocesan superintendency is not established by canon law, the position is defined by the degree of authority delegated from the bishop. While a superintendent normally exercised substantial impact on school curricula, scheduling, and other elements of the instructional program, he was seldom in years past given control over religious and lay teacher hiring, and still more rarely had any hand in parochial school finances. His authority in relation to pastors was advisory. As management authorities point out, staff personnel can have substantial impact on organizations through their professional expertise or their personal ability in getting the attention of superiors. But rarely in traditionally-structured Catholic school systems was the superintendent able to exercise substantial control over the critical areas of administrative and teaching personnel and income and disbursements within the schools.

The other officer appearing in the line and staff drawing, Figure 1, is the religious superior. Until the massive influx of lay teachers into Catholic schools in the nineteen-fifties, nuns, brothers, and priests made up by far the major part of parochial school staffs. Heads of religious communities or provinces of communities had enormous influence on the schools in which the communities served, since they assigned religious personnel to those schools. The community superior often had a tenuous relationship with the local ordinary, confined to initial contacts which culminated in a contract between diocese and community. This agreement usually stipulated the number of religious teachers and administrators the community would provide a given school and the stipend to be paid the religious by the parish. A bishop in whose diocese a community had its mother-house or "home office" would normally have more frequent contacts with the superior of that community, but these rarely resulted in systematic educational planning for the diocese.

More frequently, religious superiors dealt with pastors concerning personnel changes. Over the past twenty years these relationships have often been strained by the need to reduce the number of religious in schools. Since religious teachers' salaries are usually quite modest, cutbacks in the number of religious teachers confronted pastors with the task of both locating lay teachers and finding increased funds to pay them.

As can be seen in Figure 1, parochial school principals were usually in the unenviable position of reporting to three superiors. Areas of responsibility were anything but clear. Principals' ingenuity and diplomacy were often severely taxed by the need to reconcile obligations imposed by diocese, pastor, and religious community.

If at least the school staff's situation appears unambiguous—with reporting responsibilities exclusively directed to the principal—it is only because no drawing can convey the complexities caused for teachers by parish-to-parish differences in pastor-principal relations. Usually pastors hired and fired lay teachers, and while principals were normally consulted, decisions on staff employment were often made for reasons and by methods that were anything but professional.

One common variant from the strictly parochial pattern described above has been the central Catholic school. In the

demonstrate more specific and recognizable drawbacks.

Keeping in mind the distinction between policy making and administration, the first question concerns the role of the bishop. Is he competent to function as chief administrator and/or policy maker for a diocesan school system? So far as the bishop's capabilities as school administrator are concerned, the reply is usually obvious. The chief administrative officer of a school system should possess academic qualifications in professional education, preferably at the doctoral level, and should have a wide background of experience in school administration. Few bishops possess this training, and those who do cannot give education the time it deserves.

So far as a bishop's capabilities as policy maker are concerned, it seems reasonable to assume that he could indeed frequently function well in this role. Normally a bishop possesses the kind of training and intellectual capabilities that permit him to make valuable contributions to educational policy. But modern education is increasingly complex, and persons whose lives will be affected must more and more be allowed to participate in the process of educational policy making; these imperatives rule out the formation of educational policy by a single individual. To say bishops are incompetent to act in their former role within Catholic school systems is no criticism of many valuable contributions they have made while functioning precisely in that role; it is simply to say that neither the institution—the school system— nor the individual bishop can continue to cope with the problems imposed by the traditional monolithic structure.

What is true of bishops in relation to school systems is equally true of pastors in regard to individual parochial schools. Some pastors, it is true, are interested and able educational administrators, but their obligations extend far beyond the time-consuming duties of school operation and policy formation. No individual, no matter how talented, can have the acquaintance with sociology, philosophy, psychology, theology, curriculum, business management, law, etc., that educational decision making requires today. The theoretical and practical aspects of these disciplines demand persons

of varied experience and academic talents. It is clear, moreover, that the interests of the institutional Church, while legitimate, are not primary in education. The stake of parents and the total community in education is enormous. This argues convincingly for broader representation in policy decisions and the greatest possible competence in educational administration.

One can easily pity the school principal in traditional Catholic educational organizations. He was directly answerable to three superiors who often had little communication with one another and inadequate definitions of their spheres of authority. Since the major concern of the superintendent of schools was instructional quality; the major interest of the pastor, financing; and the strongest concern of the religious superior, the teaching staff—these three officers sometimes placed a principal in difficult and even conflicting positions. The principal possessed far too little autonomy over curriculum, money, and staffing. Quite naturally, principals resented the rigidity of diocesan-prescribed textbooks and courses of study which left little scope for adaptation to local needs. The inability of parochial school principals to obtain clear-cut budget allocations with authority to determine expenditures within that budget was another frustration. Finally, the school principal frequently wore another hat, that of local superior for his religious staff members. This created a built-in distinction between the relationship of the religious staff to the principal and that of lay staff to the principal.

In the traditional structure the staff members were at the bottom of the administrative ladder in every sense. (Perhaps "escalator" would be a better image since traffic ran almost entirely in one direction.) Rarely were formal opportunities given or channels created for teachers to exercise real influence over organizational patterns of their schools.

In this structure the diocesan superintendent of schools occupied a highly anomalous position. He was in the line of authority derived immediately from the bishop, yet rarely could he exercise that authority over nearly-autonomous local pastors. When a pastor desired advice or professional as-

sistance in his school's administration, he might turn to the superintendent's office. When he was inclined or required to seek direction concerning school income or expenditures, he usually received these directions immediately from his religious superior, the bishop.

This pastoral bypass in effect reduced the position of superintendent of schools to that of educational persuader or pleader. Not infrequently superintendents with strong personalities and professional backgrounds developed rather sophisticated techniques of exercising power without possessing real authority. In many ways this type of influence can be more effective than structurally-conferred authority, but it conferred a burden that the superintendent's personality was not always capable of meeting—more so since the superintendent was sometimes selected by the bishop with little regard for his professional training or inclinations. Because his office did not enjoy great prestige among his clerical peers but did carry with it a high level of ambiguity, the superintendent's tenure in office tended to be brief, with incumbents moving as soon as decently possible into the less frustrating role of parish pastor.

By no means the least of the principal's problems was the staffing pattern in a parochial school. Among his three immediate superiors, the one professional educator, the superintendent, was usually least involved in selecting and evaluating instructional staff. It is not surprising that religious superiors gave strong consideration to problems of relations within the religious community in making teacher appointments. But frequently what was good for the community was not good for the school. Religious personnel and diocesan clergy could not very well be fired; once a religious or priest was accepted into the community or diocese, that organization was obliged to provide for his assignments and personal needs. Remoteness—in geography as well as position and professional preparation—further aggravated principal-major superior relationships in matters of school staffing. While many religious superiors made heroic personal efforts to visit personally the schools staffed by their congregation, considerations of distance and numbers of community members, as well as the demands of other aspects of the community's life, rendered intimate personal knowledge of each school's staffing needs almost impossible.

Perhaps the most serious objection to traditional Catholic school organization is its failure to distinguish between policy and administration. The bishop was the key major figure in both processes, although his office lacked the representative aspect of school policy making bodies and the professional qualifications required of chief school administrators. The policy-administrative confusion was frequently reflected in the bishop's educational activities. He was, typically, the person responsible for initiating school building programs, arranging their financing, planning the facilities, giving overall supervision during the building process, and finally presiding over the dedication ceremonies of "his" new school. It is a testimony to the remarkable abilities of many members of the hierarchy that the failure to employ more democratic policy making procedures and more professional skills did not more frequently result in disastrous educational facilities. Such disasters, however, were not always avoided.

Again, pastors' positions in regard to their own parish schools were analogous to those of the bishops. Lack of participative decision-making processes and professional background did not prevent many pastors from making whatever decisions the bishops left to their discretion. The usually functional and moderate-cost physical facilities found in parish educational plants indicate a high level of dedication and common sense on the part of pastors. However, such qualities, even when present to a heroic degree, are not necessarily adequate to cope with modern community processes and educational needs.

The most general criticism against the religious community-owned school structure is its lack of integration into the diocesan school system. The goals of all Catholic schools in a given diocese and the needs served by these schools are sufficiently alike that all such schools should operate in one coordinated structure. While the community-

owned school often lent itself to more effective staff administration, lack of coordination in curriculum and particularly in
financing proved serious obstacles to effective school operation. While urging the benefits of alternatives to the local
public school system and of greater decentralization of the
decision making processes, Catholic educators nevertheless
found it a handicap for the Church to be operating what
amounted to several distinct school systems in a single region.
Perhaps the major drawback to the religious community's
total control of schools is the inadequacy of the financial
base in nearly all such schools. Normally dioceses and parishes assumed no responsibility for the operating expenses of
religious community schools, and frequently they did not
assess themselves for the original building project. As a result,
community schools were shut off from what is overwhelmingly the most important source of Catholic educational funding, regular or special parish Sunday collections. Virtually the entire cost of operating these schools depended upon
tuition, and despite sincere attempts to offer scholarships
(which in effect committed the religious community itself to
paying the student's cost) these schools tended quite naturally to be patronized by rather affluent families. There can, of
course, be little objection to providing and fully charging for
the education of children from such families; but restricting
Catholic education in any substantial degree to the already
privileged seems contrary to the very rationale of religiously-
sponsored education.

A more viable structure for Catholic school systems is
seen in Figure 3 on the next page.

In this simple organizational chart, policy making functions are distinguished immediately from administrative processes, and these latter operations are clearly subordinated to
and derived from policy decisions. At the diocesan level, a
board of education, as representative and democratically selected as possible, formulates overall educational plans. The
diocesan superintendent of education translates the board's
decisions into sound instructional practices. As chief pastor
of the diocese, the bishop represents an important element in

Catholic educational goals, and he should be an *ex officio* member of the diocesan board. The major religious superior delegates his responsibilities in education to a professionally-prepared member of his community, the director of education. This officer maintains liaison with diocesan education bureaus, and personnel policies are developed in cooperation with diocesan offices. This religious community official may further offer professional counsel to principals and staffs in schools maintained by his community.

Example of Current Structure

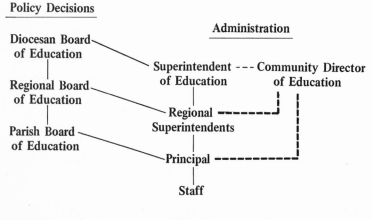

FIGURE 3

Regional boards and their corresponding administrative officers recognize the problems frequently created by immense geographical areas and different educational climates within a diocese. Frequently these boards and superintendents will function most effectively when their influence extends over the same area as that of local public school districts. Parish boards provide decentralized policy making vehicles empowered to make decisions which specify or supplement those of regional and diocesan boards.

The school principal's role with the parish board is analogous to that of the diocesan superintendent's in relation to his board. Like the superintendent, the principal is chief professional consultant of his board and is authorized to formulate school regulations that express the board's will.

If the structure cited in Figure 3 represents substantial organizational improvement over traditional patterns, it still has serious inadequacies. The presumption is that boards, through their executive officers, possess complete control over school staffs. However desirable this might appear, such control is stringently limited by at least two factors. While cooperation between religious communities and the diocesan offices offers obvious advantages in personnel practices, control of religious personnel still remains to a large extent beyond the authority of the diocese. Since superintendents and religious directors of education may not go beyond the policies imposed by their respective boards or superiors, constant renegotiating of conditions of religious teachers' services must be conducted at policy making levels. A second important modification in the suggested structure must be anticipated. Teachers in Catholic schools, like their public school counterparts, are forming associations or joining unions. Experience demonstrates that such organizations soon demand a role in the formulation of policy.

It seems fairly certain, then, that the organizational structure depicted in Figure 3 will rapidly "broaden." Line relationships will be reduced and authority for both policy and administration will be much more widely shared in Catholic school systems of the future.

OTHER EDUCATIONAL AGENCIES

Wherever appropriate in this book an attempt will be made to refer to "Catholic education," rather than the narrower frame of reference, "Catholic schools." To a great extent— perhaps to the extent of inefficiency and inequity—Catholic education usually does signify Catholic schools. Although well over fifty per cent of all Catholic children attend public elementary and secondary schools, a far greater share of personnel and financial resources is devoted to Catholic school education than to out-of-school instruction.

Each diocese has a Director of the Confraternity of Christian Doctrine, which is the body normally entrusted with the responsibility for religious education taking place outside the Catholic school. This Diocesan Director presides over a loose network of parish representatives (usually volunteers) who represent the local CCD presence.

The CCD program normally embraces two major activities: religious instruction of children who attend public or non-Catholic private schools; and adult religious education, which includes religious instruction for adults themselves and training parents to aid their pre-schoolers' religious growth.

These programs are usually understaffed, underfinanced, and underestimated in terms of their importance. However, some of these difficulties can be at least partially alleviated when parish and diocesan boards accept responsibility for planning and budgeting for all educational activities. If some diocesan CCD directors have developed well-merited suspicions of school officials, those who can bring themselves and their organizations into a coordinated educational program with the schools find their pleas for assistance receiving more attention.

While there is considerable conversation today about CCD as a total alternative to Catholic schools, most Confraternity directors would be happy to take their place as cooperators with their school-oriented colleagues in the total Catholic educational system. If announcements of the death of Catholic schools are at least premature, the fact remains that an increasing percentage of Catholic children will receive their formal religious instruction outside the Catholic school. Achieving a practical balance of needs and resources, therefore, demands that CCD and school affairs be brought under a common policy making board.

II

Catholic Education
and the Law

CHURCH LAW

The basic compendium of law for the Roman Catholic Church is the *Codex Iuris Canonici*. This *Code of Canon Law* consists of 2414 individual laws governing the structure and operation of the Church throughout the world. In the *Code,* those canons from numbers 1372 to 1383 deal with education. Insofar as they consider the administration of Catholic schools, they refer primarily to the powers of bishops, the presumption always being that the local ordinary is the primary legislator and administrator for the given diocese. So, for example, canon 1374 reserves to the local ordinary the determination of when Catholic children may attend non-Catholic schools.

Canon 1379, no. 3, stresses the obligation of Catholics, in accordance with their means, to supply the necessary resources for establishing and maintaining parochial schools. In canon 1113 it is stated that parents are bound by the gravest obligation to provide by all possible means for the religious, moral, physical, and civil education of their children, as well as their temporal welfare. Canon 1375 makes the point that the Church's schools are public schools, since "they are founded by a public authority, perform a public function, and conform to the regulations of civil authority for schools." This canon is interesting in light of current debates over public support of secular instruction in Catholic schools.

It is precisely the universal character of the *Code of Canon Law* that prevents it from being a very practical set of directions for the American Catholic educational situation. The canons necessarily deal in generalities. They must somehow be applicable to the total situation throughout the world for the Roman Catholic Church. Canon law, however, does provide certain basic support for the statements of Catholic bishops and above all for the statements of the Council of Baltimore concerning policy making authority in the Catholic school system in America. Several of these principles can be seen in the above cited canons. One very obvious one is the insistence of the Roman Catholic Church that it has some right to involvement in education. It sees itself, moreover, as having very real authority over the education of Catholics, at least insofar as it must provide for their religious instruction.

The major general source of Church legislation for parochial schools in the United States is found in the decrees of the Third Plenary Council of Baltimore, November 9 to December 7, 1884. This Council was called partly as a response to immigrant defections from the Church. These defections could, in the minds of the Church hierarchy, be traced in part to the lack of a sound Catholic education at the elementary school level. Consequently, a great part of the Third Council was devoted to Catholic education. The following excerpts give us some idea of how the bishops 80 years ago felt about the need for, and the authority proper to, Catholic schools in America. Article 194 of the Acts and Decrees of the Council states:

> The Church. . .cannot permit that Catholic parents, to whom it belongs by both divine and natural law to care for the Christian education of their children, would provide for a merely secular education. . . .[1]

---

[1]*Concilii Plenarii Baltimorenis III Acta et Decreta,* John Murphy Co., Vol. II, p. 378.

In this article the bishops of the Council rather clearly indicate two fundamental principles concerning Catholic education. One is the claim on the part of the Church of a right to deal with education. The other, a familiar theme in Catholic educational pronouncements, is that the direction of education fundamentally is the right of parents. The Fathers of the Council went on to state:

> Having weighed these matters, we do order and decree that in the vicinity of every church (where it does not now exist) a parochial school is to be constructed within two years of the promulgation of this Council and this is to be maintained in perpetuity, unless the bishop, due to very serious difficulties, grants a delay.[2]

This statement represents the fundamental thrust of the Council of Baltimore. In a few words it determined the major institutional emphasis of the Roman Catholic Church in America for the next hundred years. The attempt to carry out this decree was to influence radically the whole nature and operation of the American Catholic Church. The task of maintaining the system mandated by the Baltimore Council still constitutes by far the major monetary burden of the Roman Catholic Church in this country. As a matter of historical fact, this decree of the Council was not carried out perfectly. Some parishes could or would not establish a school within the two-year time allotment. But generally speaking, response to the decree was overwhelmingly affirmative. In the next decades there followed an enormous expansion of what had been until then only a rudimentary system of Catholic schools in America.

After establishing the principle of a Catholic school in every parish the bishops went further: they exhorted the Catholic laity to generosity in supporting these parochial schools. They urged

> ... that both the external and internal beauty and furnishings of the school be augmented, the number of instructors

[2]*Ibid.*, p. 380.

increased, the pupils be placed in classes of moderate size, and the individual classes be arranged according to the pupils' levels in the best fashion.[3]

In this exhortation one can already see an interesting attempt to establish policies and structures for the administration of a parochial school system. The attempt to define even in a general way the number of teachers, size of classes, and need for ungraded classes indicates that in educational policies there is little new under the sun.

In the next article the bishops come to a key point: the setting up of an administrative structure, a committee that would constantly examine administrative procedures as well as policy making functions. This article states:

The bishops, therefore, within one year from the promulgation of this Council, shall name one or more highly skilled priests who shall constitute a "Diocesan Examination Commission." They shall serve at the pleasure of the bishop and shall solemnly promise to fulfill the office according to the norms of the bishop and the purpose of their office. [4]

This article of the Baltimore Council establishes what we would term today a supervisory office for the parochial school system of a diocese. Authority for this diocesan examination commission and its activities revolves around the ordinary, the bishop of the diocese. The commission members may be removed at any time by the bishop; and they are obliged to report their findings to him. The same article says:

This Commission shall examine all persons who wish to teach in parochial schools, and on finding them competent shall issue them a certificate without which they may not be employed. This certificate is to be valid for five years in all dioceses. At the end of this time another final examination is to be given.[5]

[3]*Ibid.*, p. 391.
[4]*Ibid.*, p. 392.
[5]*Ibid.*, p. 393.

In these earliest school commissions we do not expect to find many functions paralleling those now exercised by diocesan and parish boards. However, it is noteworthy that there is entrusted to this diocesan examination commission a basic power of many Catholic diocesan boards today: the function of regulating and certificating teachers. Moreover, the provisions of the above article, simple though they are, suggest another current diocesan board practice, the issuing of a temporary teaching certificate upon a first examination or interview. This temporary certificate is to be followed at the end of five years by another examination leading to a permanent certificate. We see here a practice that closely parallels the issuing of teaching certificates in many states of this country. Further, the Fathers of the Council took pains to indicate the content as well as the method of both the first and the second examinations given to candidates for teaching positions in diocesan schools.

In the next article the bishops went on to establish still another educational supervisory body:

> In addition to this Commission established to examine teachers for the whole diocese the bishops should appoint for the various districts and nationalities "School Commissions" composed of one or several priests who are to examine schools. These Commissions shall visit and inspect each school once or twice a year, and shall give to the chairman of the Diocesan Commission a report for the information and action of the bishop.[6]

Again it is the local ordinary who appoints the members of the commission in question. Moreover, he is to appoint them according to various districts and nationalities; that is, these appointments are not only regional, but they allow for the existence of the "national parishes." In the nineteenth century, and even today, these parishes, drawing their members from a particular nationality group, knew no boundary lines and were virtually autonomous in terms of diocesan organization. In view of the serious ethnic controversies

[6]*Ibid.,* p. 398.

within the American Church at the time of the Baltimore
Council, such a provision was certainly realistic, for national
parishes had powerful advocates in Rome. Yet according to
the Council, even these almost autonomous parishes are to be
regulated by diocesan school commissions insofar as their
schools are viewed as an arm of the diocese and, therefore, of
the local bishop.

The composition of these school commissions is to be
entirely clerical. This decision is quite in line with the
thinking of the period, for only in the last decade have
laymen and religious commonly been considered appropriate
candidates for diocesan policy making or administrative
boards. The principal duty of these early school commissions
was to examine the schools. That is, they were to visit and
carefully inspect each school at least once a year. They were
first to transmit their findings to the chairman of the
diocesan examination commission; he then would forward
the findings with board recommendations to the ordinary for
action.

CIVIL LAW

Today the voices of public officials are frequently heard
encouraging the existence and extension of Catholic schools,
particularly in areas of great educational need. It is a little
difficult to realize that the question of these schools' right to
exist was legally determined less than half a century ago.

In 1922 citizens of the State of Oregon voted that every
child of compulsory school age must attend a public school
of his district. Two Oregon corporations, the Society of
Sisters of the Holy Names of Jesus and Mary and the Hill
Military Academy, obtained an injunction restraining the
governor (Pierce) and other state officials from enforcing the
law. The injunction was granted and, when the state
appealed, the case reached the U.S. Supreme Court. In 1925
the Court ruled the Oregon law invalid, primarily on the
grounds it deprived the corporations in question of their

businesses and properties without due process of law. The language of the decision, however, made it clear that the Court recognized that broader human rights were involved. The following paragraph from Justice Reynold's decision constitutes a sort of *Magna Carta* for parents who choose nonpublic schools for their children:

> The fundamental theory of liberty under which all governments in this union repose excludes any general power of the State to standardize its children by forcing them to accept instruction from public teachers only. The child is not the mere creature of the State; those who nurture him and direct his destiny have the right, coupled with the high duty, to recognize and prepare him for other obligations.[7]

The *Pierce* decision or, as it is often called, the *Oregon School Case*, established, if only indirectly, the right of parents to send their children to any school that meets minimal state standards. It determined, in short, the right of nonpublic schools to exist, and the right of parents to choose these schools for the education of their children.

A case decided earlier by the U.S. Supreme Court touched on limitations of the state's right to prescribe the manner and content of teaching. The State of Nebraska had enacted a law forbidding the teaching of any school subject in any language other than English, and banning the teaching of any modern language below the ninth grade.

Meyer, a teacher in a Lutheran school, was found guilty of violating this statute in that he had taught German reading to a ten-year-old pupil. The case reached the U.S. Supreme Court in 1922, and the Court decided the law was in excess of the state's power to direct its citizens' education. As later in the *Pierce* case, the Court clearly recognized the state's right to protect its interests through educational prescriptions, but it saw the statute in question as a deprivation of individual rights in an area that posed no correspondingly serious threat to the welfare of the state.

[7]*Pierce v. Society of Sisters,* 286 U.S. 510, 45 Sup. Ct.,571 (1925).

Both the *Pierce* and *Meyer* cases were landmark decisions in determining the rights of nonpublic schools to exist and to direct in large measure the content and methodology of their teaching. Another legal issue of great importance and complexity has been the degree of public support permissible for religiously-sponsored schools. No final word on this involved, emotion-charged issue has yet been pronounced by the courts. Indeed, a 1968 U.S. Supreme Court decision *(Flast v. Cohen)* virtually invites further litigation on the subject. Two cases of very restricted application, but rather substantial precedent, will be cited here.

The first is the *Everson* case, resolved by the U.S. Supreme Court in 1947. In its decision the Court upheld the right of local school districts, acting under a New Jersey statute, to provide free school bus transportation to children attending parochial schools. The Court declared that such a provision does not violate the federal Constitution.

The rationale for the Court's finding in *Everson* was the "child benefit" theory, introduced in an earlier decision concerning a Louisiana textbook law. In both cases the Court saw the aid in question as an extension of the state's welfare activities to a given group of children, not to the institutions they patronized. The majority of the Court allowed that bus rides might indeed facilitate attendance in parochial schools by children who otherwise would not enroll in them. In his majority opinion, however, Justice Black compared such results to those derived from protection by traffic policemen, fire departments, and public highways. To deprive children and the institutions they attend of such basic public welfare services, Justice Black argued, would be to show hostility toward religion, rather than the neutrality required by the Constitution.

The same opinion contained a concept due to be developed some twenty years later in another landmark decision (the *Greenbush* case). Justice Black wrote in *Everson:*

> It is much too late to argue that legislation intended to facilitate the opportunity of children to get a secular education serves no public purpose. . .nor does it follow that a

law has a private rather than a public purpose because it provided that tax-raised funds will be paid to reimburse individuals on account of money spent by them in a way which furthers a public program.[8]

In 1968 the nation's highest court ruled on the case of *Board of Education v. Allen,* popularly known as the *Greenbush* case (after the public school district whose board instituted suit). At issue was a New York law authorizing the state to supply textbooks to students attending parochial as well as public schools. The court ruled the statute did not violate the federal Constitution. The case is significant for at least two elements that extend concepts found in *Everson.* One of these is the progression from aid in a completely noninstructional category, school bus transportation, to an area intimately associated with the teaching process. Justice Black, in his dissent, rather overstates this distinction when he writes:

> Books are the most essential tool of education. . .it is not difficult to distinguish books, which are the heart of any school, from bus fares, which provide a convenient and helpful general public transportation service.[9]

If Black's effort to reconcile his opinion in *Greenbush* with his opinion in *Everson* caused him to minimize the contribution of transportation and maximize the textbook's function in education, he still correctly indicated the difficulty in drawing a line between aid to a pupil in the form of a book and assistance in the form of other learning materials, school buildings, and teachers' salaries. It is probably more than coincidence that immediately following the *Greenbush* decision Pennsylvania's legislature passed a bill providing funds directly to nonpublic schools for expenses conjoined with teaching certain secular subjects.

A second step beyond *Everson* is seen in reasoning em-

[8]*Everson v. Board of Education,* 330 U.S. 1, 67 Sup. Ct. 504, (1947).

[9]*Board of Education of Central School No. 1, etc., et al, v. James E. Allen, Jr., et al,* (October, 1967 session; not yet reported).

ployed by the Court majority in *Greenbush*. Discussion over
tax assistance to nonpublic schools tended to revolve around
the acceptability of the child benefit theory. Under this concept, aid was seen as rendered to the child as a citizen, not to
the (religious) institution that the child attended. Even to
some proponents of parochial schools, this distinction appeared to border on legal fiction. More fundamentally, it did
not recognize the essentially public character of the "nonpublic" school, and its consequent claim on public support.
Since tax aid given to school children was for school purposes
and would deal only with the educational aspect of a child's
life, why act juridically as though such aid had no impact on
the institution attended by the student? In fact, the real
focus of the *Greenbush* decision is away from the *recipient* of
aid and toward its *purpose.*

In writing the majority decision for *Greenbush,* Justice
White cited a principle enunciated by the court in a 1963
case striking down bible reading in public schools *(Abington
School District v. Schempp).*

> The test [for involvement of the State with religion] may
> be stated as follows: what are the purpose and primary
> effect of the enactment?. . .to withstand the strictures of
> the Establishment Clause there must be a secular legislative
> purpose and a primary effect that neither advances nor
> inhibits religion.[10]

Later in the *Greenbush* opinion, White gives this very
positive statement on private education's contribution to the
public sector:

> Underlying these cases, and underlying also the legislative
> judgments that have preceded the Court decisions, has been
> a recognition that private education has played and is play-
> ing a significant and valuable role in raising national levels
> of knowledge, competence, and experience. Americans care
> about the quality of secular education available to their
> children. They have considered high quality education to be

[10]*School District of Abington Township v. Schempp,*374 U.S. 203 (1963).

an indispensable ingredient for achieving the kind of nation, and the kind of citizenry that they have desired to create. Considering this attitude, the continued willingness to rely on private school systems, including parochial systems, strongly suggests that a wide segment of informed opinion, legislative and otherwise, have found that those schools do an acceptable job of providing secular education to their students. This judgment is further evidence that parochial schools are performing, in addition to their sectarian function, the task of secular education.[11]

In a "friend of the court" brief co-sponsored by the National Catholic Educational Association and several Protestant and Jewish educational agencies, this broadening of the child benefit theory is well presented.

Since fifteen per cent of all American school children are in nonpublic schools and have a constitutional right to stay there, government cannot possibly assist the secular education of those children without collaterally enhancing the secular dimensions of the schools they attend. It is fruitless to attempt a divorce between the student and the school. The government's right to reach the student necessarily involves the right to have some limited dealings, involving collateral benefits or burdens, with the school that the student attends.[12]

The *Everson* and *Greenbush* cases ratified decisions by the state legislatures of New Jersey and New York respectively. The Supreme Court has not yet ruled on the constitutionality of *federal* programs that assist parochial school education. Cases involving aid to nonpublic schools under the National Defense Education Act, the Elementary and Secondary Education Act, and numerous federal loans and grants to higher educational institutions may soon be accepted by the court. While the decision in *Greenbush* offers

11Board of Education of Central School District No. 1, op. cit.

12Brief for Amici Curiae, National Catholic Educational Association, et al, in *Board of Education of Central School District No. 1, etc., et al, v. James E. Allen, Jr., et al,* 1968.

substantial encouragement to parochial school supporters, it is by no means a clear indication that the same court will approve other categories or amounts of aid.

Education in the United States is basically the responsibility of the several states. Civil regulations that affect Catholic schools most commonly arise through state constitutional provisions and court decisions, legislative enactments, or administrative decisions of regulatory bodies, such as state boards of education.

It is obviously impossible to characterize here each state's laws and rules as they affect nonpublic schools. Very generally, however, it may be said that state constitutions and judicial decisions derived from them seldom include laws affecting the existence of nonpublic schools or the teaching carried out in them. In regard to tax assistance to these schools, however, a majority of states (38) have constitutional clauses far more restrictive than the federal Constitution. The constitutions of many states admitted to the Union during the half-century following the Civil War reflect an antipathy toward things Roman Catholic that characterized the times. It was a period of political ascendancy for the Know-Nothing Party, a nativist, anti-Catholic forerunner of the Ku Klux Klan. The constitutions adopted by many states during this period contained some version of the Blaine Amendment, named for the Maine congressman who attempted to amend the federal Constitution by a severe restriction on any kind of aid to nonpublic education. Blaine failed to achieve his purpose in Congress but realized a substantial success in seeing his proviso adopted by numerous states.

State legislatures tend to reflect special interests within each state to a greater degree than Congress. Lawmakers sometimes act as state school boards, enacting statutes requiring or forbidding certain subjects to be taught in schools, setting school holidays, or establishing conditions for teacher employment (for example, loyalty oaths). Such enactments are usually obligatory on nonpublic schools. Although court tests would probably invalidate some, they are seldom serious inconveniences to nonpublic educators.

Two areas in which state legislatures can have substantial impact on nonpublic schools are teacher certification and state-paid services. It seems clearly within the state's province to require common minimal qualifications for all teachers within its boundaries. Many states have enacted such laws, and nonpublic school teachers must conform to these certification requirements.

A second source of legislative involvement with nonpublic schools is state aid. Many state legislatures have provided for "auxiliary benefits," transportation, health care, and remedial services to children in all schools. Michigan has one of the most comprehensive such provisions. The State of Ohio in 1967 provided grants for certain kinds of assistance to all school children. Purchases under these grants are made through local public school districts. In 1968 the Pennsylvania legislature provided monetary grants to nonpublic schools for instruction in "secular" subjects.

Another point of contact between public authority and nonpublic schools is through administrative departments at state and local levels. There are numerous agency regulations concerning school building codes, fire laws, and health and safety requirements that are mandatory for all schools. The state department of instruction and its policy board may prescribe curricular offerings, minimum attendance requirements, and set standards for accreditation of schools. Whether or not the legislature has made certification of teachers generally obligatory, the state department of instruction usually has the right to insure that instruction given in nonpublic schools is adequate and approximately equivalent to that offered in public schools of the state. Far from abusing this right, most state departments, because of inadequate staffs, fail to provide very effective supervision over nonpublic school instruction.

III

Boards of Education
for Catholic Schools

TOWARD A NEW DEMOCRACY

If a single word captures the mood of the Roman Catholic Church today, it is "change." Scarcely any area of the Church's teaching and practice is immune to the challenges and reactions of its theologians, the questions and tentative answers of its clergy and laity. The spark kindled by Pope John XXIII has been fanned into a blaze of heat and light by the Second Vatican Council and subsequent efforts to develop the mood and teachings of that epochal event.

Since colonial times, the American Catholic Church has never been either homogeneous or stable enough to achieve eminence in theological studies. Just as the colonial Church had begun to assume an orderly structure, essentially French in character, waves of Catholic immigrants from Ireland, Germany, Italy, and Eastern Europe began arriving. They found the developing patterns of the American Church antipathetic, rejected them, and finally obliterated them. During the nineteenth century and the early decades of the twentieth, the American Catholic Church had to struggle simply to maintain the allegiance of these immigrants. In such an atmosphere, theological speculation does not readily flourish. To their

Western European co-religionists American Catholics appeared vigorous and loyal indeed, but religiously unsophisticated; obviously in approaching their faith they were influenced by the pragmatic, action-oriented society in which they lived.

During the Second Vatican Council this "typically American" attitude largely continued to prevail. Relatively few American bishops intervened during the Council in debates over sources of divine revelation or discussions on the nature of the Church or renewal of the sacred liturgy. But at least two documents produced by the Council bear clear evidence of American influence—the *Declaration on Religious Freedom* and the *Declaration on Christian Education.*

The characteristically American Catholic preoccupation with religious freedom derives from an almost passionate espousal of the democratic principle of government, a quality frequently noted by foreign observers. The Church has grown and prospered in the American religious marketplace. Today American Catholics are more willing than ever to espouse and promote this principle of mutual respect and friendly religious rivalry as being consistent with their theological principles and, above all, as an eminently viable approach to the old problem of church-state relations.

The handling of another traditional problem, education of the young, also has some novel aspects in the American Catholic Church. Catholic schools are not peculiar to the United States, but no religious body in any nation has succeeded as has the American Catholic Church in establishing a network of schools relatively free from governmental support or control. This system educates some 45 per cent of eligible Catholics, 14 per cent of the American school population.

The establishment of so massive a system of private education was certainly not in the mind of the Catholic hierarchy or laity during the first half of the nineteenth century. But by the latter half of that century the American Catholic Church clearly faced crises that gravely endangered its promising future. The waves of immigrants from heavily Catholic nations that had begun in the mid-nineteenth century showed

no signs of abating. Many of these new Americans found in
the Church a familiar and welcome link with their native
lands. But many more did not retain allegiance to their earlier
faith. Often, too, the children of immigrants rejected the
Church of their parents and adopted the more "typically
American" Protestant ethos and church membership. Catholic leaders perceived that a major reason for such rejection
was the defectors' ignorance regarding the possibilities of rec-
onciling their American experience with their traditional
faith. Still another reason was the strongly Protestant character of nineteenth century public schools. In that pre-
ecumenical age, teachers and curricula in public schools often
were virulently anti-Catholic.

The bishops, as we noted in Chapter II, responded to
this threat to the future of American Catholicism by ordering
the establishment in every parish of a Catholic elementary
school. They appointed committees of clergymen to inspect
and regulate those schools. But it was not long before those
committees became "paper" committees, exercising little or
no authority. Bishops and pastors tended to retain nearly full
control of Catholic schools—practically up to the last decade.
During this period, when the number of Catholic schools
increased so markedly, the laity seemed generally content to
leave direction of their children's education to their bishops,
priests, and religious.

A combination of factors in the mid-twentieth century
stimulated a substantial change in this attitude. Public school
districts were reorganizing into larger and more efficient units
and were generally upgrading the quality of their instruction.
Education was becoming increasingly complex. One contribu-
ting cause was growing emphasis on new communications
media such as radio and television; these, in turn, modified
and supplemented traditional methods of education. Finally,
Americans had become highly mobile, and community educational attitudes and expectations were no longer static.

An increasingly educated Catholic laity began to question the traditional position of cultural leadership that first-
and most second-generation American Catholics had unhes-

itantly accorded their clergy. Like other members of America's upward-striving middle class, Catholics now had an almost mystical faith in the power of "good" education. As parents, they began to question more closely the effectiveness of a school system controlled and administered almost completely by the clergy and religious communities. At the same time, parochial schools began to show signs of strain when, after World War II, they tried to absorb increases in enrollment caused by a sharply increased birthrate. This problem was intensified as the number of men and women entering religious teaching communities lagged behind school enrollments. Drawing novices from a period with a notably low birthrate, teaching communities could not provide enough teachers for their classrooms. The problems faced by these communities in attracting young men and women to religious life further complicated the situation, especially since no structure existed for supplementing their teaching staffs with adequately prepared laymen. In some instances the results were large classes and inadequate teaching, which spawned further dissatisfaction among Catholic parents.

THE BOARD MOVEMENT EMERGES

The bishops and their chief educational officers, the diocesan superintendents of education, turned to the concept of diocesan boards of education as a means of unifying parish schools and other educational programs into a more effectively functioning system. While clergymen had predominated on early boards, many dioceses now notably increased the number of lay board members because of growing parental pressures and revision of lay-clergy relations effected by Vatican II. Whereas in 1951 only four diocesan boards reported lay representation, by 1964 some 30 had lay members.

In 1966 the National Catholic Educational Association surveyed the 141 Roman Catholic dioceses then existing in the United States. Eighty-two dioceses reported that they had boards of education and, of these, 46 had lay members.

The survey also showed that teaching religious—that is, the nuns and brothers whose religious communities form a major part of the staff of almost every parish school—are commonly represented on diocesan boards, in addition to clergy and laity. In the survey, 30 dioceses reported that priests, laymen, nuns and/or brothers were members of their boards. Another four boards included priests and religious but no laymen.

By the end of 1967, a similar NCEA survey indicated that the number of diocesan boards of education in the United States had increased by 19 per cent (that is, 27 new boards). Significantly, laymen accounted for 43 per cent of all board members and religious for 16 per cent, with clergy making up 41 per cent of the total membership. Seventy-three of the boards (69 per cent) had members from all three groups, while only seven (seven per cent) were composed of clergymen alone.

This same study took the first count of area and parish boards of education. Subject to the decisions of their diocesan boards, these subordinate structures are responsible for educational policy making at the local level. The survey showed some 2100 parish boards operating in the 10,000 Roman Catholic parishes with schools in the United States—and area boards of education in 36 (or one-fourth) of the dioceses.

Another NCEA survey completed in June, 1968, indicated a total of approximately 4000 parish boards, an increase of almost 100 per cent in eight months! Unlike diocesan boards, these subordinate units are made up almost entirely of laymen.

The reasons for this astonishing growth of the board movement are both theoretical and practical.

For years Catholic educational philosophers had paid tribute to the rights in education possessed by three groups: the Church, parents, and the state. In its *Declaration on Christian Education,* the Second Vatican Council took this argument seriously and insisted that the state and parents have, indeed, real directive rights and corresponding obligations toward Catholic education. This *Declaration* both represents and augments a new philosophy of participation, which insists that the primary right of parents goes beyond the privilege of deciding which school their children will attend. Parents, it is now seen, also have a primary right over the direction of their children's education.

This concept of participation and cooperation also broadens the right of the state (better viewed as *citizens* of the local state or national community) to participate in decisions affecting the education of Catholic school children. Since these children form a large and important segment of society, that society acquires the basic right to be involved in the formation of policy affecting them.

In the *Constitution on the Church,* the Fathers of Vatican II state:

> But the laity by their very vocation seek the kingdom of God by engaging in temporal affairs and by ordering them according to the plan of God. [1]

It seems evident that policy formation for Catholic education is principally, though not exclusively, a "temporal affair." An increasing perception of the intimate relations between secular and sacred is also moving the Church toward a broadening of the educational policy making function. Catholic education cannot be viewed in the simplistic light of pastoral goals alone. The schools and other educational programs are not simply catechetical institutions; they exist to enliven and enrich secular society. But increasingly, this latter goal is seen as a legitimate and desirable objective for the Church itself.

Practical reasons, as well, argue strongly for the proliferation of boards. The Catholic community will be more willing to give moral and financial support to Catholic education if it feels involved in forming policies that govern it. Government aid also appears more likely when policy making decisions are made by a body less obviously bound to Church structure. The American democratic philosophy emphasizes

[1]Abbott, W.M., S.J., ed., *The Documents of Vatican II* (New York, 1966), p. 57.

the right of the governed to participate in decisions affecting them. From the viewpoint, then, of church-state relations and of conformity to American political patterns, lay boards of education should encourage greater tax support for Catholic schools.

A final practical reason for the growth of boards has been the realization by bishops and pastors that they cannot meet the complex demands of educational policy determination by themselves. As the *Constitution on the Church* states: "Pastors also know that they themselves were not meant by Christ to shoulder alone the entire saving mission of the Church toward the world."[2] No individual today knows as much about sociology, psychology, economics, business management, curriculum development, theology, philosophy, and political science as sound educational policy making requires. (This is not to say that all board members need be Ph.D.s; but practical aspects of applying these and other disciplines to the educational program demand persons of varied practical experience.)

For the future development of Catholic education in America, the significance of the growing board movement may not be immediately obvious. Contrary to rather common opinion, however, most important decisions concerning the government of the Roman Catholic Church—and hence of its education programs—are not made in Rome, but in the individual dioceses throughout the world, each headed by a bishop. To be sure, the bishop's authority is regulated by canon law, by decisions of general Church councils, and by infrequent papal definitions. Nevertheless, the bishop of a diocese possesses wide discretionary powers to act for the spiritual and material good of his people. In practice, the exercise of these powers entails further decentralization of authority. Although a bishop's appointments and decisions do not, in theory, depend upon the advice or consent of the clergy or laity he governs, most bishops consult with both groups. Since no bishop can be expert in all diocesan affairs,

[2]*Ibid.*, p. 57.

he establishes advisory boards composed of clergy and lay-men. Active participation in these boards is voluntary; conse-quently, practical necessity almost requires a bishop to con-sult and consider his advisers when formulating policy. Given these facts, another follows: diocesan boards of education are already influential—and will be more so—in shaping the American Church's school systems.

Area and parish boards further decentralize the formula-tion of policy and the exercise of authority within each dioc-esan system. Parish boards legislate policies for their respec-tive educational programs, while an area board within a dio-cese deals with policies affecting a number of schools and programs in the area falling under its jurisdiction; such a board may take the place of or merely supplement the func-tions of parish boards within the region. In the sharing of responsibility for policy, the relationship of both kinds of boards to the local pastor or pastors of their districts is simi-lar to that of their diocesan board to the local bishop. Typi-cally, these boards help to establish policy for the variety of educational programs that constitute a diocesan educational system: parish elementary schools, parish high schools and diocesan high schools, schools for special education (for ex-ample, for the retarded), the Confraternity of Christian Doc-trine (primarily a religious education program for Catholic students not in Catholic schools), adult education. Formal educational institutions beyond the high school level are not normally considered part of such a system, nor are private schools, that is, those owned and completely administered by religious communities or by Catholic laymen.

The chief educational officer and the diocesan board's principal adviser is the diocesan superintendent. With in-creasing frequency this officer is given responsibility for out-of-school programs, such as those in religious instruction and adult education. He is then usually entitled "Superintendent of Education." He is normally a diocesan priest, although many exceptions to this rule are beginning to appear. In the fall of 1967 two dioceses reported nun-superintendents and two had laymen-superintendents. At that time, too, 17 nuns, six brothers, and 29 laymen were listed as assistant superintendents in diocesan education offices. Since nothing in canon law provides for the office of superintendent of education, the extent of a superintendent's authority is usually determined by the appointing bishop. This is customarily modified by the traditional functions of the office in each diocese, by current practices in other dioceses, and by any synodal (local) laws relevant to the direction of educational activities.

Within the traditional organizational structure of the Church, a Catholic board of education derived its authority from a fundamentally different source than its public school counterpart. Catholic boards have commonly "represented" the Catholic public in the sense that they have presented the public's views and desires. They were not, however, fundamentally answerable to the public for decisions and were usually not selected by the members of the Church. In the past decade this situation has begun to change. The changes in education and population mentioned above have been matched by changes within the Roman Catholic Church. The Second Vatican Council has sparked a rethinking of the Church's legal structures. The Code of Canon Law is being updated; "senates" and advisory committees of clergy and laity are now established not only in Rome, but in many dioceses throughout the world. The approval of the great majority of bishops for broader sharing of policy formulation in the Church is evident from many conciliar declarations that were adopted by overwhelming majorities in the Second Vatican Council. A key statement is the following one:

> Let the spiritual shepherds recognize and promote the dignity as well as the responsibility of the laity in the Church. Let them willingly employ their prudent advice. Let them confidently assign duties to them in the service of the Church, allowing them freedom and room for action. Further, let them encourage lay people so that they may undertake tasks on their own initiative. Attentively in Christ, let them consider with fatherly love the projects, suggestions, and desires proposed by the laity. However, let the shep-

herds respectfully acknowledge that just freedom which belongs to everyone in this earthly city. [3]

In response to such declarations and to the conditions that prompted them, a number of Catholic boards today possess very real jurisdictional authority. From both within and without, the Catholic Church is today being influenced to modify its decision making structure. The resulting changes are democratizing the government of the church.

In the United States the operation of Catholic educational systems is, on the institutional level, the major preoccupation and distinguishing feature of the Roman Catholic Church. The parish school will typically consume from one-half to two-thirds of parish income. The overwhelming majority of nuns and brothers are directly engaged in Catholic education, and nearly all the clergy are at least indirectly engaged. In this country then, changes in attitude and in the authority structure of the Roman Catholic Church will be felt most vitally in diocesan educational systems. The board movement is one result.

BOARD OF EDUCATION POWERS

Unfortunately, relatively little information is now in print about Catholic boards of education. A large body of literature exists concerning the powers and operations of public school boards, but in drawing analogies from the experiences of public boards considerable care should be exercised: the differing philosophies and legislative frameworks of public and church educational systems make caution necessary in comparing them or in offering one as a norm for the other.

Some people find it hard to believe that boards in parishes or dioceses are "for real." Considering the way in which authority has traditionally been exercised in the Church, this is hardly surprising. Unquestionably, some of the several

[3]*Ibid.*, pp. 64-65.

thousand boards now existing were intended as little more than window dressing: a passing acknowledgement of the Church's current concern for collegiality and lay participation. But this need not be the case, and a majority of boards do indeed possess substantial control over policy making.

The authority a Catholic board of education possesses may be of three orders or grades:

1. *Advisory.* This board discusses school affairs and offers counsel to the bishop or pastor. In a 1966 survey of diocesan boards[4] 25 per cent of the respondents described their board as purely advisory.

2. *Legislative, subject to approval.* This board formulates policies for the schools by resolutions that the bishop or pastor either approves or vetoes. In the 1966 survey 53 per cent of the diocesan boards said they possessed this kind of jurisdiction.

3. *Legislative and autonomous.* The bishop or pastor agrees in advance that any decision made by the board, within the limits of its authority, will automatically bind the school system. In the 1966 survey 15 per cent of the diocesan boards said they possessed this authority.

(In the above-mentioned survey, seven per cent of the respondents failed to supply information on these points.)

It is worth noting that a number of superintendents responding to the diocesan board survey indicated that they felt a board could never be more than advisory. They argued that ultimate legal control of all diocesan institutions is in the hands of the ordinary, and they did not believe this authority could be delegated. Apparently this posed no problem for at least 10 bishops, who, in fact, delegated final jurisdiction to their boards.

In comments they appended, those superintendents who described their boards as "legislative, subject to approval" indicated episcopal vetoes of board legislation were very rare. Several of these indicated preference in principle for a com-

[4]Deneen, James R., *Status of System-Wide School Boards in Catholic Dioceses in the United States,* Doctoral Dissertation, Indiana University, 1968, 123pp. (No systematic survey of parish boards' authority has been made to date.)

pletely autonomous board, but felt the current arrangement represented a reasonable accommodation to the facts of life in their diocesan authority structure.

It also seems noteworthy that those boards possessing purely advisory powers included a disproportionate share of those on which clergy made up a majority of the membership—and were those that met least often.

When the superintendent-respondents were asked the kind of authority they thought their boards should have, eight per cent indicated a desire for advisory boards, 56 per cent for legislative boards, subject to the approval of the bishop, and 31 per cent for completely autonomous boards. (Five per cent did not indicate their preference.)

In the recommended diocesan board constitution found in *Voice of the Community,* the authors say:

> All decisions of the Board of Education shall be binding on the Superintendent of Education; the Office of Education; all subordinate Boards of Education; and the pastors, principals and staffs of the schools and catechetical programs within the Diocesan system. [5]

In the constitutional model for parish boards found in the same publication it is stated: "This Board is a regulatory body. . .subject to such regulations that proceed from the Diocesan Board of Education." [6]

Obviously, the above remarks place the authors clearly on the side of those who advocate autonomous boards. This position seems most consistent with the arguments advanced above for the existence of boards.

It is probably true that any board is better than none, but when people today are asked to participate in decisions that deeply affect their own and their neighbors' lives, they naturally prefer to believe that their considered counsel will be decisive under democratic procedures. Normally, if not

---

[5] *Voice of the Community: The Board Movement in Catholic Education,* Superintendents' Committee on Policy and Administration, National Catholic Educational Association, The Association, Dayton, Ohio, 1967, p. 14.

[6] *Ibid.,* p. 31.

invariably, a board that confines itself, or is confined, to advice-giving, does not feel the same sense of involvement as one possessing final legislative authority. Anything less than authority to formulate policy, subject to extremely rare episcopal or pastoral veto, does not seem consistent with recognized rights of parents and the community.

If this argument for strong board control is valid, it implies a substantial change from the traditional roles of bishop and pastor. These positions are not identical. Both have a strong role in Christian education by reason of the teaching authority they possess in the area of religion, but the bishop is the administrator of the diocese and head of the corporation that owns the schools. As long as this is so, the possibility exists that any delegated control over the schools may be rescinded by the ordinary who granted it or his successor. A solution soon to be adopted in some dioceses will probably be to transfer title of ownership or lease school properties to boards of education. Failing this, a bishop may pledge his acceptance of all diocesan board decisions, and may authorize and require the same attitude from his pastors.

It is sometimes difficult to persuade laymen to accept responsibilities that the clergy formerly bore completely. It is even more difficult for many bishops and pastors to transfer these responsibilities, with corresponding authority, to the laity. But this transfer can be made, and there are persuasive arguments today that it must be made if Catholic schools are to maintain their vigor.

BOARD OF EDUCATION MEMBERS

A great deal of concern revolves around the composition of diocesan and parish boards. What qualities are desirable in board members? How should they be selected? How long should they remain in office? While these questions are subordinate to that of board authority just discussed, they are still important. The *Handbook for Committee Members of Friends Schools* suggests the following questions be considered in evaluating a prospective board member:

1. Is he a person whose views on life and on education are such that his presence will enrich the committee and, either directly or indirectly, contribute to the spiritual health of the school?

2. Is he free to attend meetings regularly and to work on sub-committees?

3. Has he a real interest in the school? Is this interest likely to grow?

4. Is he willing to take on work and does he complete a job he has undertaken? Is he discreet and able to keep confidences?

5. What additional attributes will he bring to the committee: experience in business? in a profession? in community service? as a homemaker? Is he outstanding for his judgment? for initiative? for leadership? [7]

Prospective board members who meet all or most of these requirements will be rare, but as a board will usually embrace a wide range of opinions, so may it include a diversity of specialized abilities and interests.

Whether to elect or appoint board members is an old controversy in public education. As a matter of practice today, the majority of diocesan board members are appointed, while for parish boards some sort of elective process is more common. There are some arguments favoring appointment. It may result in a higher quality member than would be realized through more democratic processes. This might be particularly important in the initial years of a board. It is, moreover, quite difficult to arrange diocesan-wide elections or even to conduct this kind of democratic process in a typically large urban parish.

If an election process is decided upon, this could be, for diocesan boards, a result of balloting by parish or regional

[7]*Handbook for Committee Members of Friends Schools,* Philadelphia Yearly Meeting of the Religious Society of Friends, Philadelphia, 1968, p. 12.

board members. In a given parish, the home-school association or the entire parish might vote. As was pointed out above, however, the area and population of some parishes make general elections rather difficult. Home-school associations, on the other hand, usually represent only parents of school children. Despite the difficulties, some sort of election process seems preferable in selecting board personnel. Their increased acceptability by members of the parish or diocese and their sense of obligation toward the electing body make the elective method of choosing board members preferable.

Constitutional statutes of parish and diocesan boards typically establish a limit of two three-year terms of office for members. Unquestionably, a danger exists that boards will become closed and stagnant if new members are not brought in. However, studies of board effectiveness indicate that members who have served from four to six years were significantly more effective than those who had served three years or less. If the board is elected, at least two terms of three years each should be permitted.

Vocational backgrounds of board members can severely limit or notably expand the board's contribution. In *Voice of the Community,* it is recommended that the pastor be the only ex officio member of the parish board. It is urged that no special criteria for board membership be established, but that two categories be ineligible to serve—salaried employees of the parish and board members or employees of another school or school district. While the authors of *Voice of the Community* recognized the valuable contributions professional educators could make to parish boards, they felt that the importance of maintaining the distinction between policy making and administration makes it inadvisable for Catholic school employees to serve on parish boards. In what seems a much weaker argument, they suggest that public school board members or employees might experience conflicts of interest. While the parish school principal, like the diocesan superintendent, is ineligible for board membership, he should always be the chief executive officer of his board.

Studies of diocesan boards show notable imbalances in

vocational categories of board members. The 1966 survey referred to above showed that men made up 82 per cent of the membership; persons under 30 years of age, only one per cent of the total membership; Negroes, four per cent of the diocesan board membership; and non-Catholics, one per cent of diocesan board membership. Diocesan priests at that time comprised 48 per cent of the members, with representatives of male religious communities comprising five per cent, and representatives of female religious communities comprising eight per cent. Laymen comprised 28 per cent of the membership, and lay women 11 per cent.

To a great extent these boards were not made up of "laymen," as distinct from either clergy and religious or professional educators. It seems reasonable to believe that this handicapped the members in their effort to function as true representatives of the community and confused the distinction between policy making and administration.

Many boards, particularly at the diocesan level, appoint standing committees to make recommendations for policy in a single area of educational operation. Such a practice is commonly discouraged in studies of public and nonpublic boards. The arguments for this are that a policy making board should primarily be made up of generalists, with their specialties lying outside the field of professional education. The board should depend on the system's administrative staff for its investigations into specific professional education areas. Work on standing committees, moreover, tends to be extremely time-consuming with resulting discouragement and absenteeism on the part of board members.

IV

The Basic Functions
of a Catholic Board

DETERMINING THE BOARD'S RESPONSIBILITY

It is impossible to speak sensibly of a board of education's
responsibilities before its authority has been clearly determined. The board must find answers to several questions.
What is its charge? What powers does it possess? What are the
community's educational needs and expectations? Only after
the matter of the board's jurisdiction has been thoroughly
explored and settled to the satisfaction of all parties concerned may the board proceed with its duties. A corollary of
this requirement is the importance of a written manual or
constitution and bylaws in which the board's powers and
procedures are spelled out in some detail.

In attempting to clarify its policy making responsibilities a board should substantially involve its executive
officer in the discussion. The obligation of translating board
decisions into programs rests primarily with this officer. He
should command personal or staff resources for the detailed
development of every educational area for which the board
will legislate. As the superintendent or principal has a basic
responsibility to keep the board informed of developments
generally in education and specifically within its own system,

so is the board obliged to instruct its executive agent about its span of interest and control. When a board drifts aimlessly or becomes involved in matters outside its competence, its educational agent is paralyzed in trying to act sensibly and decisively, and the entire educational process suffers.

ESTABLISHING PERSONNEL POLICIES

It is axiomatic that a board's relationship with its administrative officer is the most important personnel issue the board faces. Indeed, so important is it that it will be treated at length in a later chapter of this book. Here we shall consider only the board's function in relation to nonadministrative staff personnel.

> ... a board should set the policies for appointing staff members. . .thereafter the administrator should make all appointments in accordance with these policies. If a board approves of appointment qualifications, salary levels, classification plans, and number of employees by grade authorized in the budget, then it has far more control over the process than by approving lists of these appointments and promotions. [1]

The above statement describes sensible restrictions along with the obligations of boards toward personnel placement. It rules out as well an unfortunately common practice, especially among parish boards, of personally recruiting and interviewing candidates for teaching positions. This is obviously the duty of the board's professional staff.

Salary schedules in schools or school systems are usually based upon two considerations: seniority and educational background with some consideration normally given for special responsibilities (for example, coaching, or supervising the yearbook). While some public school districts claim success for "merit pay" plans, there is little evidence that teachers'

[1]Parkman, Francis, and Springer, E. Laurence, *The Independent School Trustee* (Boston, 1964), p. 15.

associations, administrators, and even boards can agree on a measurement of teacher productivity as a basis for determining pay. The problem of rewarding the able and industrious has always proven difficult for bureaucratic organizations. Even apart from dangers of inequity, measuring teacher effectiveness is undoubtedly difficult. Still, it seems a difficulty with which boards and representatives of the instructional staffs must deal. Possibly some models and experimental plans could be devised for a given district. Certainly the failure of such plans can be guaranteed by (1) formulation and imposition of a plan that was not devised cooperatively by board and teachers, or (2) failure to understand that standards of business and industry cannot be applied to school sytems without modification.

When Catholic school policy makers think of staff salaries, their inclination is to center on the problems posed by and for lay teachers. The difficulties in determining adequate compensation for teaching religious are, however, frequently much more complicated. In computing religious personnel costs to the parish or diocese, factors beyond the usual token salary must be considered. Among such considerations are housing, including maintenance and supplies, money and services received from drives, sales or informal contributions, and transportation and medical insurance.

Every parish and diocesan board should request of the religious communities a professionally-prepared statement of their requirements. In terms of salary such requirements must, of course, take into consideration the educational preparation of a community's members, care of the aged and sick, and support of other religious community apostolates. The religious teachers' and administrators' salaries should then be compared with the regular (lay) salary scale for comparable personnel. The difference—between the value of the services rendered by the religious and the amount actually paid their communities—should be gratefully reported as "contributed services." This procedure not only helps the school or system to understand better its true operating cost, but shows in dramatic and understandable terms the debt of gratitude owed by the community to its teaching sisters, brothers, and priests.

Salary schedules, along with other benefits and general conditions of employment, should be established at the diocesan level. Some recognition, however, must be given to disparities of income, living costs, supply of teachers, and local public school scales within a diocese. The best procedure for a diocesan board may be to set such policies in very general terms or to tie them to some local condition—for example, to require that Catholic school salaries be kept on a par with, or at some specific percentage of public school salaries.

A retirement age for all teachers and administrators should be set by the diocesan board—if possible, in conjunction with other dioceses of the state. Such cooperation makes possible statewide pension and retirement procedures and benefits, and discourages a flow of elderly teachers into a given diocese or area. Work conditions should be set in general terms by the board. If board members feel the need for detailing some of these conditions, for example, defining teaching load (by number of periods or hours per day or week), this should only be done upon recommendation of the board's administrative officer. Usually, specifics of such issues are better left to administrative regulations.

Every employee of a school or school system should work under a signed contract with the board. While this procedure is common for lay teachers in Catholic schools, contracts with religious are usually signed by the bishop or pastor and the religious community superior. There is some feeling today that religious teachers should sign individual contracts with their employing diocese or parish. This, it is argued, would more clearly demonstrate the professional educational nature of the teacher's role and his acceptance of the obligations as well as rights conferred by that role. Others feel the value of this procedure is largely symbolic and is outweighed by a loss of religious community consciousness on the part of individual religious and the diocesan or parish board that employs them. The question of individual contracts becomes highly significant when teacher negotiations are considered. Increasingly, Catholic school teachers are organizing in associations and unions to negotiate conditions of their employment. A hotly-debated issue is whether religious teachers can or should join these associations. Some religious communities discourage or flatly forbid such membership; others are more permissive—with the result that some of their members normally join.

This whole issue of collective bargaining in Catholic education is exceedingly complex. Some dioceses, most notably Philadelphia, have been forced to deal with militant teacher associations on a city-wide basis. In Chicago, diocesan authorities have been drawn into controversies between teachers and religious community-owned schools.

In general, personnel policies should be the first item of business for Catholic school boards. The actual or imminent existence of teacher associations should be recognized, accepted, and encouraged. Whether at the diocesan or local level, the board must be the employer with whom the teachers negotiate. When these negotiations involve a formal contract on an area or diocesan basis, the board should employ the services of persons experienced in personnel negotiations. The position, and usually the background, of the superintendent render him ineligible for this task. It is always difficult, and often impossible, for the superintendent to assume his proper role as leader of the schools' instructional staff if he has functioned as a representative of one party in sometimes bitter and highly polarized employment negotiations. For more routine relationships between staff and board, however, the superintendent or local principal would seem an appropriate and capable mediator.

Discussion of Catholic educational personnel must include some comment on the future of religious communities. Prophecy is as easy as it is unreal, but what is happening today in many religious teaching orders at least suggests strongly some developments in the immediate future. The number of teaching sisters, brothers, and priests is declining annually. The most sensational and publicized reason is the departure of many from religious community life. Much more significant, however, is the very substantial decrease in the number of those who are entering religious life. One obvious conclusion drawn from this single fact is that laymen will continue to increase in numbers and importance within the Catholic system even if the number of students within the system remains stable or shows continued moderate declines.

In addition to the ominous shadow cast by reduction in the number of novices and seminarians, factors within the school system and religious communities are also causing the proportion of religious teachers to decline. Long overdue limitations on class size are being enforced in many dioceses, so that more teachers are required for the same number of pupils. Within the communities, an increasing number of religious have taken advantage of opportunities for greater personal choice and opted for social work, pursuit of advanced degrees, the Newman apostolate in non-Catholic colleges and universities, and sometimes for teaching in public schools.

Speaking before the 1968 Conference of Major Superiors of Men, the Reverend Felix F. Cardegna, rector of Woodstock College, a Jesuit seminary in Maryland, predicted that many religious will move away from formal communities and pursue the goals of secular Christianity in a professional environment. These persons and others like them, whom we would today designate as laymen, may very well come to make up the overwhelming majority of teachers in Catholic schools. The attitudes they bring to the school and the satisfactions they receive from it may, within a decade, determine Catholic education's future.

FINANCING THE EDUCATIONAL PROGRAM

There is certainly a place in educational literature for a definitive study on Catholic school finance, but this will not be it. Probably the best recent study bearing on this problem is that done by Dr. Anthony E. Seidl in his book *Focus on*

Change (New York: Wagner, 1968). Much of what Dr. Seidl says about budgeting, accounting, and school business management should be required reading for Catholic board members and administrators, and there is no point in duplicating or inadequately summarizing his material here.

A basic question with which Seidl deals only in passing is the critical one of how Catholic education can be financed. The sociologist, Father Andrew Greeley, argues that much of the current controversy over the allocation of Catholic educational resources is irrelevant. Although it is commonly said that Catholic schools must choose between the inner-city and the suburbs, Greeley argues that it is quite possible for the schools to serve both—neither totally nor perfectly, but still providing a true and effective Catholic presence in both environments.

He feels the enormous parental demand for Catholic schools in the suburbs will generate adequate financial resources from tuition, supplemented by parish funds. Inner-city Catholic education would have to be supported basically through subsidies from the diocese. A problem with Greeley's argument is that many dioceses possess relatively meager income resources apart from their parishes. In effect, the suburban parishes would be supporting both suburban and inner-city education. It may well be argued, however, that if suburban schools are closed, inner-city education will not be notably enriched. It is at least questionable whether suburbia's Catholics have achieved a level of social concern that would cause them to give generously to educational fund drives from which their own children would derive little apparent benefit. The Catholic community, which has to date borne almost the entire cost of its school system, undoubtedly is showing signs of the strain caused by rising enrollments and per-pupil costs. But as Greeley and others have pointed out, it remains to be demonstrated that support for well managed Catholic schools that produce results desired by parents will not be forthcoming.

In the January, 1968, issue of *Marriage* magazine, Father George Elford points out that better financing for

Catholic education involves at least two factors: more efficient fund-raising methods, and equalization of education based on need rather than local (parish) financial ability. Father Elford notes that fund-raising experience among Protestant churches demonstrates that an annual pledge campaign to meet a cooperatively-prepared and published budget is the most effective method of financing. The churches have discovered that late April or early May seems the most opportune time for such a campaign. These lessons seem appropriate at both the parish and diocesan level, since such a campaign would provide the diocese with a source of funds to promote better quality education in less affluent parishes.

Besides the Catholic community, another source of financial support for Catholic education is what may generally be termed the civil community. Today sectarian schools at all levels—collegiate, secondary, elementary—receive financial assistance from a wide spectrum of local, state, and federal agencies. That assistance is severely limited in amount and scope. Legal and sociological obstacles make increases in such aid difficult to predict, but Congressional leaders of both political parties foresee an enormous increase in federal aid to education in the near future. During the last decade it is precisely at the federal level that Catholic schools have met the fewest legal barriers in obtaining tax support, and precedents set by existing laws such as the Elementary and Secondary Education Act suggest that these schools can anticipate receiving, at least indirectly, future federal assistance.

Several states have recently passed laws giving aid in modest amounts to church-related schools, and, as was seen in Chapter Two, the State of New York's textbook law, under which approved texts are lent to nonpublic school children, has been upheld by the United States Supreme Court. In June, 1968, Pennsylvania enacted legislation providing for monetary payments on a per-pupil basis for Catholic schools. Ohio and Michigan have laws enabling nonpublic school children to participate broadly in "welfare benefits" connected with education. Among such benefits are transportation, health services, and many remedial classes. In several other states, efforts are being increased to test the severe restrictions of their constitutions and determine the feeling of citizens about the use of state funds for church-related schools.

Another source of funds Catholic administrators have scarcely probed is the business and industrial community. One would expect the orientation of this group would make it a leader in demanding the continuance of nonpublic education, which not only promotes educational diversity, but represents enormous tax savings at the elementary, secondary, and collegiate level. Very few nonpublic educators, however, have made a reasoned and sustained appeal to the common sense of the business community. School taxes comprise an enormous share of the tax burden of companies and their individual managers and employees. If only a small share of the tax savings realized through the existence of nonpublic schools are allocated to those schools, the savings—and the schools—can continue.

One Catholic educator who has made just such an appeal is Father Niles J. Gillen, superintendent of schools, Diocese of Joliet, Illinois. In September, 1967, he began in one county of the diocese a systematic effort to explain the significance of Catholic schools in that area, and what their loss would mean in terms of educational and financial impact. Father Gillen limited his appeal for aid to the four Catholic high schools of Will County, and suggested three possible approaches to the business and industrial community. One was a formula based on the number of employees. The second was a formula based on the tax savings nonpublic schools realized for a given company. The third was substantial voluntary contributions from concerned individuals. Before support could be obtained from large industries, broad local backing had to be demonstrated. Within relatively few months a systematic campaign raised $150,000 in pledges and contributions from strictly local sources.

What it all adds up to is the overwhelming need for good planning in Catholic education. This is a fundamental task for a board of education: to determine, with its administrative staff, the goals of the system, what programs can best achieve these goals, how budgetary limitations must modify them, and how the agreed-upon program can be carried out and evaluated.

In 1968 the National Catholic Educational Association sponsored in five major cities a series of seminars on techniques of long-range financial planning. Only when these and similar planning techniques are taken seriously by Catholic educational policy makers, will reasonable answers to financial questions in Catholic education be possible.

EVALUATING AND PLANNING

Boards of education have an obligation to make regular reports to those they represent. Those to whom a board most obviously owes this duty are parents, students, faculty, the Catholic community, and the general civil community. What these groups are most interested in and have a right to know is how well the schools are carrying out their objectives. Reporting, then, implies evaluation.

Not that board members carry out the evaluation themselves. This is properly done through the administration and/or outside resources. But the evaluators must be commissioned by the board and their work must relate to the goals approved for the educational system by the board. A detailed description of the evaluation process can be found in Chapter Eight. Some recent and current studies of Catholic education will be indicated here, along with a brief description of their purposes and procedures.

Two such studies have been conducted on a national level. *Catholic Schools in Action* is the report of the Carnegie-sponsored study directed by the Office for Educational Research at Notre Dame University; *The Education of Catholic Americans* contains findings by Andrew Greeley and Peter Rossi for the National Opinion Research Center. Both studies were published in 1966. They do not make light reading, but they contain almost indispensable background information for Catholic board members.

One of the most interesting evaluative studies at the diocesan and parish level is "Alternatives in Catholic Education" (ACE). In 1967 the Archdioceses of Indianapolis, Indiana, and Louisville, Kentucky, and the Diocese of Evansville, Indiana, agreed to share costs and resources in determining the status, and planning the future, of their educational programs. The ACE plan was fundamentally a self-study on the part of each parish in each of the three participating dioceses. The director appointed to carry out the study was the assistant superintendent of Catholic schools in Indianapolis, Father George Elford.

The ACE plan involved four phases. The *study* phase, in which a report on the educational program of each parish was made, was drawn up according to forms and directions provided by the study office. Pastors and parish counselors were also asked to submit information on parish finances, and a parish team of laymen studied population and enrollment trends. The second phase of the study involved *information dissemination* and *discussion.* A series of newspaper articles and radio and television interviews informed the communities of the problems and potentialities in Catholic education. A special booklet, *New Directions in Catholic Education,* was distributed free of charge to every Catholic household. Parish and regional discussions on the future of Catholic education were held throughout the dioceses. The *opinionnaire* phase followed, with every Catholic household asked to respond to a lengthy questionnaire covering its views on various issues and possibilities in Catholic education. The questionnaire, which was designed by the Catholic Education Research Center at Boston College, included models of educational alternatives with questions following each model. Following analysis of reports from local discussions and extensive computer analysis of opinionnaire replies, *reporting* began to diocesan and parish boards and to the general public. With this information in hand, the boards were able to begin more systematic planning for the future of their Catholic educational programs.

A somewhat different approach was taken in the Arch-diocese of Denver when it commissioned a study of its school system. The design, operation, and reporting phases of the Denver study were conducted through the Office for Educational Research at Notre Dame. Teams of experts in education and allied disciplines studied the status of the arch-diocesan school system and reported on its condition and potentialities.

The Archdiocese of Dubuque, Iowa, initiated a study with one very specific purpose in mind: to determine the feasibility and acceptability of large-scale school consolidation. The archdiocesan school office, under the direction of the superintendent, Bishop Loras Watters, designed the study to insure maximum participation of parishioners who might be affected by school consolidation. The result of the study was a dramatic decrease in the number of small school units, with resulting efficiencies in school operation. Careful attention was paid to the problem of transportation of pupils from parishes whose schools were closed.

In the Diocese of Portland, Maine, a well-designed evaluation of the school system was carried out with local resources under the direction of the superintendent of schools, Father Charles Murphy. Results of the study, completed in 1967, were quickly translated into educational decisions by the diocesan board of education. Policy making and administrative units were reduced in size, and more regional autonomy was realized.

The most extensive Catholic educational study proposed to date is now underway in the Archdiocese of New York. A committee, many of whose members are non-Catholic educators, gives policy directions for the study. The administration and operational planning for the study are under the direction of Dr. Robert Binswanger of Harvard's Graduate School of Education. The New York evaluation is to embrace all phases of Catholic education within the Archdiocese, and the committee is commissioned by Archbishop Terence Cook to provide not only information and suggestions for procedural improvements, but to give basic re-directions of educational goals where these seem advisable. The Archdiocese has pledged financial support to the extent of half a million dollars over the projected two-year duration of the study.

Numerous other dioceses, large and small, have made such studies in very recent years, or are now planning for them. Among these are such different areas as: Saginaw, Michigan; Baltimore, Maryland; Dodge City, Kansas; Boston, Massachusetts; Grand Island, Nebraska; and a cooperative study proposed for the six dioceses of Michigan.

It should be emphasized that these studies are both local and diocesan in scope, with diocesan reporting possible only after each parish or individual school has carefully examined its own operation and capabilities. It cannot be said too often or too strongly that intelligent board action at the diocesan or local level depends upon factual information, including information about community attitudes.

Boards interested in initiating such studies may obtain information from the National Catholic Educational Association in Washington. Many dioceses that have completed the studies are willing to share information; this will avoid the waste of time and money that would be involved if each diocese undertaking such a study were to try to "invent the wheel" for itself.

V

The Board and Administrator
Work as a Team

SELECTING THE ADMINISTRATOR

The relationship between the board of education and the administrator—the superintendent in the case of a diocesan board and the principal in the case of a parish board—is of crucial importance. The administrator is at one and the same time the board's executive officer, professional adviser, persuasive leader, loyal follower, mouthpiece, listening post, and whipping boy. It is to the advantage of both the board and the community to exploit to the full the resources represented by the administrator.

Boards blessed with good administrators and administrators blessed with good boards, who know how to pull together, can work wonders for education. Smooth, productive cooperation between board and administrator is no accident. There are well recognized and commonly accepted rules for guiding that relationship, and we shall examine them.

Yet it remains true that defining the relationship is no easy matter, particularly for Catholic boards of education. The Catholic board movement is still feeling its way in this area, and a spirit of reasonable give and take and mutual respect is essential.

For example, the administrator, be he superintendent or principal, should be regarded as an employee of the board. In many places, however, the outlines of this employer-employee relationship are far from clear. On the diocesan level, it has been customary in the past for the local bishop to appoint the diocesan superintendent, with little or no attention paid to the preferences of the diocesan board of education. The report on boards prepared by a superintendents' committee of the National Catholic Educational Association suggests instead that when the bishop has chosen a candidate for the post, "the board should have the right to accept or to refuse."[1] It also recommends that when a board is not satisfied with the work of its superintendent, it should have the right to ask that he be replaced, although allowing the bishop "due time so that he might protect the priest in his other ministerial responsibilities."[2]

Again, since the principal is to be regarded as the employee of the parish board, the board should technically have the right to retain or dismiss him. The difficulty here, of course, is that most principals are members of religious communities whose assignment is at the discretion of religious superiors. In this situation, the NCEA superintendents' committee mentioned above recommends only that "the Office of Education should lay down rules and guidelines for the use of parish boards in this matter"[3]—which is perhaps about as specific as anyone can be on this complicated matter just now. Obviously, a good deal of discussion and trial and error (probably including some howling mistakes) will be necessary among boards, diocesan authorities, and religious communities to work out smooth procedures.

In passing, it is worth noting that the growing trend toward lay administrators in Catholic education—including lay superintendents and lay principals—may be a major bless-

[1] The Superintendents' Committee on Policy and Administration, *Voice of the Community: The Board Movement in Catholic Education*, p. 9.

[2] *Ibid.* Similarly, if the bishop wishes to reassign the superintendent, he should time this "so as not to disrupt the work of education."

[3] *Ibid.*, p. 30.

ing here. It is possible to deal with lay administrators simply as professionals, unencumbered by priestly or religious status. Procedures developed by boards in dealing with lay administrators should provide useful guidelines in developing procedures for dealing with clerical and religious administrators.

Whatever say the board does have in the choice of administrator, the exercise of its responsibility here is one of the most important tasks confronting it. When the administrator is wisely chosen, the board's trials and tribulations are substantially reduced.

It is to be hoped that the selection process will not occur too often, particularly in the case of diocesan superintendents. While, as was noted in an earlier chapter, the turnover rate among superintendents has been dismayingly rapid in some places, increasing emphasis on professionalism—both in the choice of a superintendent and in the nature of the duties and powers assigned him—will reduce this.

Nevertheless, boards will sometimes be called on to participate in the selection process. In that case, it is necessary for the board to have criteria for the job at hand. There are, naturally, no foolproof ones, but a board that knows the sort of administrator it wants will be in far better shape than the board that has to rely on hit-or-miss methods and purely subjective criteria ("he seems like a nice fellow").

The board should be prepared to consider basic questions about the kind of administrator it is looking for. It will need a statement of qualifications desired—saying, for example, whether the board wants a person with a master's degree in school administration (a minimal requirement for a diocesan superintendent), a master's plus, or a doctorate or its equivalent. Further, the board will want to state the experience it desires in a candidate and any special personal qualifications suggested by the character of the parish or diocese involved.

In the past, the question of individual contracts for Catholic educational administrators scarcely arose. Religious communities contracted with bishops to provide certain educational personnel and services in dioceses; lay teachers might (or might not) receive contracts to teach in Catholic schools. But contracts for priest-superintendents and nun-principals simply did not enter into the picture.

If it would be an exaggeration to say that all this has changed today, it would also be an example of serious short-sightedness to fail to see that it is now in the process of changing. The arrival on the scene of the lay superintendent and the lay principal provides part of the reason for the change. The understanding of the relationship between board and administrator (whether priest, nun, or layman) as that between employer and employee provides another part. Whether or not your board now has a formal contract with its administrator, it is safe to predict that sooner or later it will.

When it does (if it doesn't already), be prepared to offer your administrator a contract of from three to five years. Better still, make the contract renewable annually for the purpose of extending it to full term.

There are several important advantages in longer contracts. They are more likely to attract capable people. They make for stable, courageous leadership over reasonable periods of time because of the increased security of the incumbent. They permit greater continuity in the program. Too rapid turnover works to the detriment of the educational program, since no man can do his most effective work until he becomes acquainted with the community he is to serve. When an administrator leaves, he takes with him a valuable store of knowledge and background—which his successor can replace only slowly. Staff morale is likely to be higher if changes do not come too frequently.

UNDERSTANDING THE ADMINISTRATOR'S TASK

There is little question that superintendents and principals occupy positions of great importance. The demands made upon them are heavy.

For example, personnel administration—which involves

hiring, firing, recruiting, training, supervising, assigning, scheduling, and conciliating—can be a full-time job, a job made more difficult today by the stepped-up tempo of educator militancy (one might even call it "class consciousness"). Educator militancy manifests itself in the actions of teacher organizations that talk of—and sometimes carry out—sanctions or strikes, that insist on negotiations or collective bargaining concerning wages and working conditions, that emphasize "you" or "they" against "us." Teachers can no longer be taken for granted or pushed around; consequently, personnel administration will demand more and more of the administrator's time and skill in the future. And while militancy has been most evident in the ranks of public school teachers, the same tendencies are present and growing among Catholic school teachers, including many religious. Unfortunately for the administrator, he is likely to find himself caught between the power of the board on the one hand and the power of the teachers' organizations on the other.

Another of the urgent demands facing the administrator is the increasing complexity of curriculum content and teaching methodology. We can draw a parallel here to what happened in the medical profession after the publication of the great Flexner Report in 1911. Until that time almost anyone could practice medicine—and often did. Most homes boasted a "Doctor's Book," a kind of everyman's guide to the diagnosis and treatment of disease. Mother would get out her copy whenever one of her children got sick. She treated them with mustard plasters, epsom salts, camomile tea, sulphur and molasses, and patent medicines. The distance that the science and practice of medicine has come in the intervening years is astonishing. Even physicians must rely on other physicians who are specialists. And specialists must, like Alice in Wonderland, run breathlessly just to stay in the same place—professionally, that is.

Like medicine after 1911, the field of education is moving boldly ahead, too. The educational administrator is hard put to try to keep abreast of new developments in such fields as physics, mathematics, biology, modern languages—

developments that demand major alterations in the curriculum. Even religion courses, once so firmly "set," are today in a state of flux as new ideas and new topics for exploration come on the scene.

As a result of research, our understandings of the learning process—and consequently our teaching methodology—are changing. The difference between the skilled teacher of today and a generation ago is about as great as the difference between today's skilled M.D. and the layman of 1911 practicing medicine with the "Doctor's Book." Not everyone recognizes the change that has taken place. And there is more to come from the almost frightening findings of research on the influence of drugs on idea creation, motivation, and memory. It is not wild to predict that tomorrow's teachers will be able to control conditions of optimum learning much as today's farmers control conditions of optimum growth in plants and animals.

What all this means, of course, is that the industrial/technical revolution, which has transformed almost every other field of human endeavor, is at last moving into the field of education.

Again, the administrator feels the pressure. He can no more keep up with *all* the developments in *all* the subjects taught in a modern educational system than can a hospital administrator be knowledgeable about all the specialties of a medical staff.

So much for internal pressures. The external pressures on the administrator—those coming from the community—are just as formidable. Here are some examples:

Resistance to increased costs. The public often does not seem to care what is done in education, so long as it means no more money out of anybody's pocket. Just let costs go up, and people scream. The administrator, they all too frequently believe, is the cause. It was he who conned the board members into letting him spend all that money!

Stepped-up roles of the state and federal governments. No need to argue as to whether the influences are good or evil. The fact is that laws and regulations must be observed, grants must be applied for, the money must be spent for the purposes intended, accounting must be specific, and reports must be drafted and submitted. More pressures. . . .

Special interest group activity. One needs only to list a few of the active groups: the National Association for the Advancement of Colored People, the John Birch Society, the American Legion, and, of course, ultra-conservatives and ultra-liberals within the Church itself. Each of them seeks to direct the schools along a path leading toward its own organizational or ideological goals. Each considers its position sound. And the administrator feels the pressure. . . .

What does the administrator do? His central task is to make decisions, or to guide the process of decision making, with specific goals in view. Choosing or deciding always precedes action. His problem, then, is to maximize the probability that action resulting from the decision will lead to desired goals.

The task that confronts him, both experience and research show, is enormously complex. A "sound" decision must be followed by a "sound" course of action if the educational enterprise is to be advanced toward its goals. Results, then, depend upon the kinds of choices made and upon the kinds of action processes that follow. The complexity grows out of the number and nature of forces to be seen, weighted, and allowed for as they bear on both processes. It is clear that the work of educational administration is of great social significance. The education of children, of people, is a *cause* to which the administrator frequently becomes dedicated to the exclusion of selfish ends. Many are the administrators who have suffered because a budget was reduced, or an important segment of the educational program was cut out. They could have sat back and accepted the decisions resignedly. But they almost never do so.

Whether your board participates in selecting a new administrator or inherits one, he should be given authority equal to his responsibility. To do any less is unfair to the administrator and endangers the well-being of the educational program.

According to best practice, the board of education should include in the written, officially adopted handbook on policies and regulations some guiding principles for determining the administrator's responsibilities and authority.

Here, for example, is a job description for the superintendent as adopted by a board of education:

Functions: Superintendent of Education

General Statement. *The superintendent of education is the executive agent of the board. He shall provide professional leadership in the diocese, and shall administer and supervise the educational program in such a way as to provide sound learning opportunities for the students.*

In addition to his statutory duties, the superintendent of education shall, under the direction of the board and in accordance with its policies, have general supervision of all activities under the control of the board. He shall make such rules and give such instructions as may be necessary to carry out the policies of the board.

In the case of an emergency not suitably covered by any policy of the board, he may exercise the full power and authority of the board and report his action to the board not later than the next regular meeting.

He shall attend to all necessary details of administration and shall faithfully perform all such other duties required of him by the board.

Functions of the Superintendent in Relation to the Board. *Except when matters pertaining to his own employment are under consideration, the superintendent, unless excused by the board, shall be present at all meetings of the board and its committees. He shall have the privilege of taking part in all deliberations.*

He shall prepare and submit to the board recommendations relative to all matters requiring action by the board. He shall place before the board necessary and helpful facts, information, and reports; and on matters requiring the tech-

nical assistance of specialists, he shall be responsible for making available the advice of qualified persons. Payment for such services shall be approved in advance by the board.

He shall at all times keep the board informed relative to the activities operating under the authority of the board. He shall inform the board relative to the educational philosophy and practices in the educational program.

a. Nomination of Employees. *The superintendent shall make it of paramount interest to secure competent teachers and other employees for the educational program. For each vacancy he shall select the ablest and best qualified candidate available.*

The election of any employee of the board shall be valid only if made on the nomination of the superintendent.

The board, at its discretion, may reject any nomination made by the superintendent. In the case of such rejection, it shall become the duty of the superintendent to make another nomination as soon as practicable.

b. Assignments and Transfers. *The superintendent shall make such assignments and such transfers in assignment of employees as the interest of the service may require, reporting his action to the board for information and record.*

c. Dismissals. *The superintendent shall report to the board the case of any employee whose service is unsatisfactory. He shall recommend to the board what he deems to be appropriate action.*

The superintendent shall make recommendations to the board concerning any employee who in his judgment shall be dismissed or whose contract should not be renewed.

d. Staff Communications to the Board. *All communications to the board or to any committee of the board from staff members shall be submitted through the superintendent except as otherwise provided. All such communications shall be referred to the board and to the proper committee at the next regular meeting by the superintendent, with or without recommendations. Nothing in this paragraph shall, however, be construed as denying the right of any employee of the board to appeal directly to the board.*

e. Meetings of Employees. *The superintendent shall hold such meetings of teachers and other employees as he may deem necessary for the discussion of matters concerning the improvement and welfare of the educational program.*

The superintendent shall keep the public informed about modern educational practices, educational trends, and the practices and problems in the educational programs of the diocese.

Responsibilities. *The superintendent in his discretion may delegate to other employees of the board the exercise of any powers and the discharge of any duties imposed upon the superintendent by vote of the board. The delegation of power or duty, however, shall not relieve the superintendent of final responsibility for the action taken under such delegation of power or duty.*

a. Study of Education. *The superintendent shall keep himself informed by advanced study, by visiting other systems, by attendance at educational conferences, and by other means, of modern educational thought and practices. He shall keep the board informed concerning educational trends.*

b. Study of Local Programs. *The superintendent shall continuously study problems confronting the educational program, and from time to time shall present to the board factual data with proper evaluation relative to such problems. Together with the staff, he shall continuously study and revise all curriculum guides and courses of study.*

c. Buildings and Sites. *The superintendent shall make recommendations on the following matters relating to buildings and sites:*

1. The location and size of new school sites and of additions to existing sites.

2. The location of new buildings on school sites.

3. The plans for new school buildings.

4. All appropriations for sites and buildings.

The superintendent shall also make recommendations on improvements, alterations and changes in the buildings and the kind of equipment.

d. Curriculum and Textbook Adoption. *The superin-*

tendent shall recommend to the board for its adoption all courses of study, curriculum guides, major changes in texts and time schedules to be used, and shall also submit to the board any radical departure from established policy or one that requires increased expenditures.

e. Records. *The superintendent shall insure maintenance of adequate records for the educational program, including a system of financial accounts; business and property records; and personnel and enrollment records. He shall act as custodian of all contracts, securities, documents, title papers, books of records, and other papers belonging to the board.*

f. Transportation. *The superintendent shall make recommendations to the board concerning the transportation of pupils in accordance with the law and the requirements of safety.*

g. Use and Care of Property for Educational Use. *The superintendent shall provide suitable instructions and regulations to govern the use and care of properties for educational purposes.*

The basic division of labor, developed by boards and administrators who have worked together successfully in the past, is that the board *legislates* and *evaluates* and the administrator *executes.* The line of demarcation is not always clear, especially to an observer sitting in a board meeting. But keep in mind that the board is an official entity only while it is in a called meeting. Once the board has adjourned, the only executive authorized to carry out the board's mandates and to run the educational program is the administrator. For example, the board adopts a policy on the community use of school buildings; the administrator puts the policy into effect. The former is a *legislative* function; the latter, an *executive* one. Later, the administrator may report to the board how frequently and which groups are using school facilities, what the effects of those uses have been, and perhaps make recommendations for changes. The board considers the report carefully and decides whether the effect of the policy is good or bad. In this case, the board *evaluates.* The arrangement is similar to that found in a well run industrial organization where a board of directors employs a president and staff to run the business in accord with board policies.

Naturally the board and administrator will have common problems. There will be ample reason for each to confer with the other. As technical adviser to the board, the administrator keeps the board well informed about the condition of the system and proposes the adoption of needed policies. The board, on the other hand, may make suggestions to the administrator as to administrative procedures. This is as it should be. But when a consensus is reached, then the lines of authority and responsibility should be clearly understood; the board legislates and evaluates; the administrator executes.

In brief, when board members are called upon to select or approve a new administrator, they should do so carefully according to tried and tested procedures. When an administrator is selected, give him encouragement to do his best. Support him with an extended contract and a written definition of his relationship to the board and staff—and give him your strong and vocal backing in the community. Then use him to the full and expect him to produce.

UNDERSTANDING THE BOARD'S TASK

Let us look first at what makes for an effective board member.[4]

An effective board member knows that he does not make decisions as an individual. He makes them as a member of a unit, the total board of education. That means that he:

1. Subordinates his personal interests for the good of the board.

2. Accepts and supports majority decisions of the board.

3. Identifies himself with board policies and actions.

[4]Adapted from a memorandum dated July 14, 1964, by Dr. Daniel E. Griffiths for the New York State Council for Administrative Leadership entitled, "The Effective School Board Member."

4. Identifies the significant problem revealed in the evidence presented to him in a board meeting.

5. Recognizes problems that demand board action and sees the difference between them and those that should be solved by the administration.

6. Suspends judgment until the facts are available.

7. Develops alternate solutions to problems.

8. Makes up his own mind once all the evidence is in and the discussion is over.

9. Understands the need for teamwork between the board and the administrator.

10. Understands the desirability of delegating administrative responsibility to the administrator.

11. Supports the administrator in his authorized functions.

12. Stays out of administrative functions such as visiting classrooms, purchasing materials, interviewing teachers and the like.

13. Knows that a board should have written policies and sees that the board uses them.

The effective board member constantly studies his job to learn more about it. He reads the publications given to him by the administrator. He prepares carefully for each meeting by reading the material sent out with the agenda. He attends board of education institutes and conferences designed to make him better informed and takes responsibility for his own improvement as a board member.

Conversely, both experience and research show that an ineffective board member:

1. Allows personal interest to take precedent over the needs of the educational program—for example, by seeking special favor for his own children, manipulating board affairs for business profits, seeking employment for friends and relatives, or seeking status or personal aggrandizement.

2. Shows inability to understand or respect the executive function of the administrator. Such a board member cannot see the difference between policy making and administration and dabbles in both without understanding that he

is making a mess of his board work.

3.   Abuses those with whom he does not agree and uses insulting tactics to gain his way.

4.   Lacks courage. Such a board member gives in under pressure and is unable to stick to his guns when faced with opposition.

Experienced board members can help newly elected or appointed ones in getting acquainted with their jobs. Here are some suggestions:

1.   Immediately after his appointment or election, the new board member should arrange for a conference with the administrator to receive an overall picture of the job and suggestions for additional sources of information.

2.   He should be offered this book and any additional available readings on the work of the board member that present a balanced view of the job.

3.   If enough time elapses between appointment to the job and formal installation, he should be invited to attend board meetings as an observer. If this is done, the new member will lose less time in assuming his share of the burden once he is installed.

4.   He can be invited to informal chats with present and past board members about the task that faces him.

5.   He should be given membership in any available board of education associations along with a schedule of meetings of interest to him.

6.   He should be given subscriptions to one or more of the periodicals that deal with the problems boards face.

7.   He should be given a copy of the policies, regulations, and bylaws manual of the board, together with back issues of the board meeting minutes for two or three years.

8.   He should be encouraged to review the annual reports of the administrator for the past several years. There may be other publications of the system that should be included in this category.

9.   He should be offered copies of any special studies of the system that may have been made, such as a school survey, a report of a special consultant, or a report of any

recent appraisal by the state department of education.

10. He should be invited to attend conventions of board associations with his expenses paid by the board. Attendance at the conventions cannot be advocated too strongly. They add a new perspective to the job. By comparing notes with board members from other areas and by listening to analyses of educational problems by state and national authorities, a new member gets valuable help in finding solutions for local problems.

11. He should be urged to visit other systems, especially those known for their excellence. His visits should be planned with definite, limited objectives in mind. He will not have time to see everything. For example, one visit might stress elementary school building facilities; another, school sites; another, board of education operations; another, faculty remuneration and fringe benefits.

No one should get the opinion from reading the foregoing that the effective board member and the effective administrator are supermen. They are not. The point is that proper planning, orientation, and instruction can help each board member and each administrator rise to heights of effective performance not otherwise possible. Just as good coaching can make athletes out of boys and girls from the general population, so "good coaching" can make interested and dedicated persons become fine board of education members who can work effectively with their administrator.

VI

Governing Your Schools
Through Written Policies

THE THREE-WORD VOCABULARY

On several occasions thus far, we've made passing reference to an all-important concept in board of education operations. We're referring, of course, to *policy making.* Now we'll examine that concept in depth. . .and point out how a board, by applying it, can achieve the highest level of effectiveness.

Let's begin by considering three key words.

Policy. Rule. Bylaw.

This little three-word vocabulary will help you distinguish clearly between the board's job as policy maker and the superintendent's or principal's job as administrator and rule maker. It represents months of thought and years of testing on the firing line of actual board operation.

The difference between a *policy* and a *rule* is like the difference between the board's job and the superintendent's or principal's job. Although one sometimes shades into the other, life is simpler and happier for boards and administrators who can tell them apart and who can honestly say—*vive la difference!* A *bylaw* is generally recognized as a horse of still another color. Its special meaning becomes clearer after we understand the first two.

So let's take them one at a time—policy, rule, bylaw.

A policy is a guide for discretionary action. It must be narrow enough to give clear guidance to the administrator as he makes decisions. But it must be broad enough to leave room for him to use his own discretion in making decisions.

Policy making is the board's job. A policy is the board's way of saying what *it* would do if it were sitting behind the superintendent's or principal's desk all day long. Of course, the board cannot sit behind the desk and so it cannot know the knots he has to untangle. The board must tell him what to do, yet not tie his hands utterly. This is what a policy does. Policy making is a way—probably the only way—for the board to give the administrator the sense of direction he needs without neutralizing his professional skills.

Example: Suppose board members have been hearing remarks about teachers not being on hand before or after school to help individual children who are having trouble with their homework. The board discusses the matter with the superintendent or principal, who investigates and finds there is no consistent pattern. The board decides to express the wishes of the community on the matter. It might adopt this policy statement:

> Teachers shall be available to assist individual children outside of the regular school day.

Or it might go further:

> All instructional personnel except those supervising student group activities shall be available to assist individual children both before and after scheduled class hours.

Or even further:

> All instructional personnel shall be regularly available to assist individual children for a substantial amount of time both before and after scheduled class hours.

But that is far enough. By that time, the administrator will have the idea and can take over himself.

Each of these statements is "a guide for discretionary action." The intention of each is clear, but even the narrowest still leaves leeway for the administrator to decide exactly what to require of the teachers.

A rule is a specification of a required action. It tells exactly what is to be done, and it usually tells who is to do it and when. It leaves little room for individual judgment.

Rule making is the administrator's job. It is one of the methods he uses to carry out the board's intentions as expressed in board policies. The administrator makes rules when he wants to leave little or no room for individual deviations—when he wants to be positive that certain things will be done by certain people at certain times. A *rule* is a type of *administrative regulation.*

Example: Suppose a diocesan superintendent were making rules (administrative regulations) to carry out the above policy statements on teachers' duties before and after school. He might, after conferring with the principals and the teachers, make this rule:

> All classroom teachers should be in their rooms fifteen minutes before classes begin each morning to help students who need special attention.

Or this one:

> All classroom teachers should be in their rooms fifteen minutes before classes begin each morning and fifteen minutes after classes end each afternoon to help students who need special attention. All special teachers who work directly with children should follow the same plan in the buildings in which they are scheduled for the day.

> Teachers who coach or who sponsor other student activities are not expected to be available to help individual students while those sponsored activities are in session.

Or even this one:

> All classroom teachers should be in their rooms fifteen minutes before classes begin each morning and fifteen minutes

after classes end each afternoon to help students who need individual attention. All special teachers who work directly with children should follow the same plan in the buildings in which they are scheduled for the day.

Student group activities should not be scheduled during these times since teachers will not be available to supervise them. Teachers should inform students and principals should inform parents of the hours during which teachers will be on duty to help individual students.

A bylaw is a rule—a rule governing the board's internal operations. Like any other rule it specifies required actions, leaving little room for individual judgment.

Making bylaws is one method the board uses to hold itself in line. Good bylaws build stability into board operations and prevent the excitement of a moment from pushing the board into behavior it may later regret.

Example: Suppose the board has decided that although it does not wish to divide itself into standing committees, it still needs an occasional temporary committee to do a short-run job. To provide for this, but to prevent the self-perpetuation of "temporary" committees, the board might adopt the following bylaw:

No standing committee shall be appointed to perform any of the board's functions.

Temporary committees shall be appointed by the president only upon the official authorization of the board. The president shall specify the functions of all such committees, shall regularly request reports to the board concerning their activities, and shall dissolve them when their specified functions have been completed.

Again, suppose the board wants to make certain it spends a fair share of its time studying the instructional program. Suppose also that it knows how often last-minute emergencies and business matters get piled in with the agenda of such meetings. It might adopt the following bylaw:

The board shall meet at 8 p.m. on the first Tuesday of each month to handle business affairs and matters requiring board action.

The board shall meet at 8 p.m. on the third Tuesday of each month to receive and to discuss information concerning the instructional program. No official action on any matter shall be taken at such meetings.

Once you master the three-word vocabulary, the way is clear to begin the actual policy writing process.

POLICY WRITING

If you feel tempted to say that you are too busy to formulate policies just now, start immediately! Nothing saves time like policy making itself. The very first policy the board adopts will actually increase its control, reduce its work load, and free the administrator—just a little of each. That will make a bit of slack in which to write and adopt another policy, which will in turn make a little more slack for another, and then another. This process picks up speed, and before long the board will find itself not only able to formulate policies, but also able to handle the other matters that once absorbed it—both in less time than it formerly spent on the second job alone.

Put it another way. Policy making is not something *in addition to* what the board is doing now. It is *instead of* something the board is doing now. And it is more important. Here's how to begin:

DON'T appoint a committee.

DON'T write to a lot of other schools for their handbooks.

DON'T go through the old minutes.

DON'T collect a pile of policies and bring them in for board adoption.

DON'T think you have to start big.

DON'T expect to get finished in six months—or a year.

Some of these things can be done later. None of them will help much at the beginning (though if you've already done some of them, nothing is lost—you can easily go on from where you are).

On the other hand—

DO explain to the staff what is being done and why.

DO choose the person who is going to write your policies (ideas on who this might be are offered later).

DO ask your executive officer to prepare and distribute blank looseleaf notebooks to board members, principals, and other key personnel. When a new policy is adopted, mimeographed copies should be distributed to all those holding the notebooks, and the notebooks should be located so that all board and staff members can refer to them as necessary.

DO take one of the *next* problems the board is facing—one it will tackle at its next meeting.

DO find the issues in the problem—the "either we do this or else we do that" choice.

DO list the policy elements—considerations the administrator would have to keep in mind in making the decisions needed to put the eventual choices into effect. They might be: cost, safety of pupils, morale of staff, reaction of parents, effect on rest of program, or whatever has to be considered.

DO discuss the issues and the policy elements with the staff and with the other persons affected.

DO discuss the issues and policy elements at a meeting of the board, taking into consideration the reactions of persons who will be affected by the policy.

DO have the policy writer draft a statement of board viewpoint for adoption at the following meeting.

DO have the board amend and adopt the statement. Don't try for perfection—chances are it will have to be changed later anyway.

DO have the administrator make—on his own authority *without* board adoption—any specific rules needed to execute the policy.

DO send copies of the policy statement and of any administrative regulations to all persons holding the notebooks.

Continue the series of steps in the policy making process described above. As each new problem appears on a board meeting agenda, see what choices can be made in solving it, choose the solution best for your situation, and adopt a statement guiding the administrator, but leaving him elbow room to maneuver as he sees fit.[1]

Keep your eye on the *future* problems that demand policy decisions from the board. Policy writing devoted to recording *past* decisions will not give you enough help today to seem worthwhile, and you may decide to give it up. But policy writing used as a *means of solving upcoming problems* will do so much good and save so many hours, that you will have the wish and the time to dip into your history and record the usable decisions of your past as guides to your future.

Policies come from problems. Board of education problems come from people—people who have a stake in educational programs and want them to do something for them or their children. Thus boards find it necessary to take policy positions on the sort of problems posed, for instance, by:

1. An association of school secretaries seeking higher salaries.

2. A diocesan official wanting to schedule retreats for students.

3. A state Civil Defense agency urging the schools to teach more about air raid attacks.

4. A citizens' committee cautioning board members to screen all textbooks before purchase.

5. A graduating class wishing to hold the senior prom in a downtown ballroom.

6. An auditor criticizing the board for spending funds for student scholarships.

7. Parents insisting that more be done for the gifted.

8. A home and school association asking the board about parents giving Christmas "tips" to school bus drivers.

9. A neighboring parish seeking help in educating its

[1]Some of this room will be in the form of leeway to make the specific rules he thinks are needed to make the policy work.

students while its new school is being built.

10. A group of parishioners asking that a fund drive be delayed until the new students are on hand.

11. A teacher organization asking the board to allow professional growth credit for summer travel.

12. A group of parents demanding that their children be transported the short but dangerous distance across a major highway.

After the policy making process is well underway, there is some value in sifting old records for original statements of policies that are in effect currently, but are not written in convenient form. The same sort of search may turn up usable administrative rules.

Chances are that the explorer of dusty documents will find a wealth of rules—many contradicting others—but few real policies. However, if someone can remember the original *purpose* of a rule—the sort of problem it was intended to solve—a new statement of its *intent,* cast in policy language, may be worth the board's adopting today.

There has perhaps never been a speech, an article, or a book about policy making that did not caution boards against copying the policies of others. Considering this, how much real help can a board get from studying policies and rules originating in other school systems?

Certainly the *rules* of others cannot be copied in their content, although their form and organization may be worth duplicating. True *policy* statements, however, present a somewhat different picture. Since they express a general relationship between broad policy elements, they are worth the policy writer's attention, first, for the elements they list, and second, for the relationship established between those elements. The first should help any policy writer as he searches for the factors he should consider in drafting a statement on a specific topic. The second may be of less value since it is less transferable from one situation to another.

One person should be chosen to put policies on paper. This assures consistency of style and lets the writer develop skill and speed at the job.

For best results, he needs a knowledge of the language, some facility in writing, and enough free time to do the work. He also needs full access to board minutes and all records. He must have a thorough knowledge of local educational programs, close contact with the administrator, and a sense of the kind of problems educational administrators meet every day. Finally, he must attend board meetings to hear policy discussions if he is to express accurately the intent of the board.

Some member of the administrative staff—the superintendent or principal or an assistant, preferably—will probably come closest to meeting these qualifications. Next would come some other administrator, or perhaps a teacher who could spare the time to attend meetings and do the writing, possibly for extra compensation.

The board clerk or secretary in some places will have the necessary qualifications. What he is most likely to lack is a sense of the freedom the administrator needs under any board policy. Lacking it, the clerk will have trouble drafting satisfactory policy statements.

An interested citizen, perhaps an unusually endowed former board member or other person close to education, might be found to have the time, the devotion—and the detachment—needed for the job.

Present board members come at the bottom of this list of possible policy writers because they stand at the top of a more important list—the list of persons responsible for providing leadership and control for education.

WHY THE BOARD SHOULD NOT MAKE RULES

Rules must be broken to meet unusual situations. If the board insists on making rules, it usually gets one of two results:

1. People—administrators included—break the rules right and left because they have to act now and they can't wait two weeks for the board's permission; or

2. They deluge the board with requests for exceptions to the rules because of special circumstances in this or that case. Either way, the rules do not give the board the control it wants and needs.

Let's be specific. Suppose the board in a fast-growing diocese has adopted this rule:

> The maximum number of pupils permitted in an elementary class will be 35.

On registration day all fifth grade classes fill up to 35, and then two more fifth graders enroll. The board does not meet for three more weeks. What is to be done? The thinking of the school principal or superintendent will probably run like this: "The board did not mean for that rule to make us either hire another teacher and move a class out into a rented building or put the fifth grade on double session just because of one or two extra children. The board means 35 to be a rough maximum—desirable, but not rigidly fixed. We'll put those two fifth graders in with the regular classes and see what happens next fall. It's what the board would want us to do." That's right. It is.

Now the process of thinking illustrated by that decision is important. In many circumstances, people—administrators included—will guess what the board *intended* when it made a given rule and they will follow that *intent* even though they may break the rule.

This is what is happening when a parish organization asks for ash trays at a Saturday meeting in the school cafeteria although the sign clearly says NO SMOKING. And it is why they get them! It is what is happening when an experienced teacher after years of remarkably loyal attendance is sick one day over the board's limit and the administrator forgets to deduct her day's pay. [2]

Proof that these exceptions were within the board's unexpressed *intent* when it adopted the rules lies in the fact

---

[2]This is also what is happening when a person drives through a red traffic light on a quiet street at three o'clock in the morning, or when he parks his car beside a NO PARKING sign after a severe snowstorm.

that the board will approve of them if it hears about them later.

Conclusion: the board can do no better than to express its intent in policy language in the first place.

People affected by policy decisions should help make them.

This fact is well established in experience and thoroughly documented in professional literature.

The *process* by which policy questions are analyzed, studied, debated, and settled is critically important. At every opportunity this process must bring together the two major parties—the public and the professionals. It brings them together to stand on a common ground and to talk a common language. Policy language *is* just such a common language, nontechnical and easily understood. It expresses intent without specifying method. Thus it can be used by both laymen and professional alike to reach, express, and record agreement on the purposes of the educational program.

Long before the board adopts policy positions on critical matters, all those who are affected or concerned should have helped shape the board's thinking.

Teachers, assembled in general meetings, represented on faculty councils, or divided into study committees, can pool their best thinking to suggest board policies that will create the conditions needed for good teaching.

A local teachers' association, acting in a certain sense independently of the individual positions of its members in the system, can aid substantially on all policies and especially on those affecting the status, compensation, and welfare of professional personnel.

Principals, perhaps meeting as members of an administrative cabinet, can easily draw upon their rich background of experience in day-to-day administration in recommending the adoption of policies that make sound operational sense.

System-wide councils of teachers and administrators can learn to advise the board on keeping a healthy balance in the total pattern of educational activities.

Members of the nonprofessional staff can be expected

to help formulate policies in the areas of their responsibility.

Students, principally through their organizations, like to be invited to express their opinions about policy choices that concern them directly.

The home-school association (or its local equivalent) through individual building organizations, regional study groups, an overall executive council, or public meetings, provides an excellent forum to debate policy issues and to formulate opinions for the benefit of the board.

Citizens' committees, in all their variegated forms, are increasingly playing major roles in studying educational problems from the viewpoint of staff and community and in recommending policy positions to the board.

Community organizations will have valuable ideas about educational operations that the board should consider.

Other parish or diocesan bodies can keep the board alert to broader issues and perspectives.

Individual citizens—speaking to board members on the street, commenting at public hearings, or petitioning the board to grant special requests—should be looked to and listened to for policy suggestions.

Finally, the administrator's advice and counsel, incorporating the breadth of viewpoint that only he can possess, regularly goes to the board on every policy matter.

One of the best chances to involve the teachers comes when the administrator and his staff develop rules to carry out the policy. This may occur before or after the board adopts a policy, depending upon whether the administrator wishes to show the board in advance the rules he plans to use. A policy means little to teachers until administrators start deciding how to exercise the discretion left them by the board. At this point everyone becomes deeply interested. Faculty councils, teachers' association committees, representatives of nonprofessional groups, and others should be called upon as appropriate for advice and suggestions.

Contrary to what is often recommended, however, you will not find it necessary to give the full-scale "involvement" treatment to all policy formulation. Some policies that you are considering will fit so well with local traditions and staff expectations, that a quick review of policy drafts by citizens and teachers will be sufficient. Others you can adopt solely on the advice of the administrative staff, particularly those that affect limited administrative or business problems.

One feature of the recommended notebooks is especially valuable here: their loose leaf design stands as permanent notice to everyone that changes are expected. You may want to strengthen this impression with a preface in the front sections of the books. State, for example, that anyone left out of the original formulation of a policy or rule can come in later with his new ideas—it is never "too late."

INTERNAL BOARD OPERATIONS

Some phases of the board's own internal operations should be regulated by the specific, firm, hard-to-change rules called *bylaws. Bylaws establish the structure of board operations.* They are needed to set regular meeting dates, times, and places, to regulate the official appointment of board committees, to assign duties to officers, and to outline routines for carrying on meetings and elections. Put a comprehensive list of bylaw topics in a separate section in the back of the policies and regulations notebook. Label this section BYLAWS OF THE BOARD.

There are other phases of its own internal operations for which the board will want to establish, both for itself as a corporate body and for its individual members, certain *policies* as guides for discretionary action. *Policies of this type describe the process of board operations.* They may be needed to describe the procedures the board wishes to use in meetings, the sort of jobs for which it wishes to create board committees, the kind of functions it wants to assign to its officers, and the general relationship it wishes individual members to maintain with the administrator and with other educational personnel. To preserve such decisions, set up another section labeled INTERNAL BOARD OPERATIONS.

File your action record here.

Federal, state, canon, and synodal laws give every educational program a framework of limits. Boards and administrators must know these limits and must keep within them when formulating local policy.

Once a policy is written, the person reading it needs to know which are the externally-set limits and which are the local limits. They should not be scrambled together in the same statement.

On the other hand, trying to quote law, whatever its source, is something like trying to put an octopus into a briefcase. You hardly know where to start, you can't get it all in, and you may be leaving out the most important part.

The answer lies in using legal references to footnote local policy statements. This places them in front of the reader just when he needs them, distinguishes between legal and local limits, and allows for comprehensive references in a few lines of type. When an occasional law is brief and clear—and uncomplicated by court interpretations or ecclesiastical regulations—it may be quoted as part of the footnotes.

Most authorities suggest that policy manuals should be reviewed and amended annually. Boards that try an annual revision discover that this is too seldom to keep the books up to date, and yet too often for a serious review of all policies.

The concept here presented, based on nearly a score of years of carefully tested experience (and the observation of a national landscape littered with out-of-date policy manuals), is entirely different. Written policies are looked upon not merely as recorded history, but as working guides for day-to-day administration. As such, they are tested every time they are used and must be changed immediately if found faulty. Otherwise they cannot guide administrators properly. The same thing applies to the set of administrative regulations with even greater force since it is more specific and thus more restrictive.

The recommended loose leaf notebooks fit this conception. Frequent changes are expected. Think of policies and rules as forever tentative. Follow them loyally while they stand, but always be ready to improve them.

Policies on the books when new members take office presumably have the full approval of the board unless and until the board acts officially to change them. Formal re-adoption of the whole handbook should not be necessary. However, if a new board wishes officially to readopt existing policies, it should not suspend the entire set while it examines each statement, but should keep the set in force to stabilize operations even while it considers amendments. In the absence of other instructions, the administrator should assume that all policies on the books continue in effect.

Any amendments the board wishes to make should be adopted and circulated one by one just as with new policies.

Incoming members will find that a close study of the board handbook of policies, administrative regulations, and bylaws can give them a focused picture of board thinking and a headstart on knowing what aspects of school operation they would like to improve.

Now it is time to consider how a board of education can best operate when it has mastered the three-word vocabulary. This matter we shall deal with in the next chapter.

VII

A Design for More Effective Board Meetings

TOWARD EDUCATIONAL LEADERSHIP

Precious are the few short hours the board of education meets, perhaps the most precious the community owns. When the community places its educational aspirations in the hands of the board, it also assigns it the community's future. With so much at stake, the people deserve and expect the finest quality of educational leadership the board can produce during its few concentrated hours of existence. For their part, most board members want nothing better than to meet (and match) this challenge.

Yet the hope of the community and the ambition of the board are too often frustrated by the flat actuality of meetings that are petty, quarrelsome, and time-ridden on the one hand, or stale and uninspiring on the other. Most of the trouble springs not from a lack of sincere effort by the board or the administrative staff, but from a shared ignorance of what it takes to hold a truly effective board meeting.

Nevertheless, many communities do have good board meetings and—to some extent because of good meetings and the thinking patterns that good meetings create—good board members. They get them by techniques that almost any other board can either copy or adapt.

In this chapter we will describe those techniques in detail—and on the basis of them, propose a program that, if followed, will help your board operate with the maximum possible effectiveness.

The program is founded on two assumptions.

First, the board should concentrate on performing its basic functions. We believe that a board of education's chief purposes in meeting—that is to say existing—are:

1. To establish the objectives of the educational program.

2. To select policies that will guide the administrative staff in working toward those established objectives.

3. To review the decisions made by the administrative staff in carrying out the board's policies.

4. To evaluate the effect of the board's policy decisions in achieving the board's objectives.

5. To perform officially those specific actions required of the board by its constitution.

The program we propose focuses the board's attention on these purposes at all times.

Second, we believe that a board meeting can be truly effective only if it is structured so as to take into account— and encourage the flowering of—the human element. Board meetings, after all, are meetings of people. Most of the things that are true of people at other meetings are true of board members at board meetings. These are some of the important things—always present but often forgotten—to be remembered about a man at a meeting:

Before the meeting he has to prepare himself if he is to contribute his share. He needs a clear idea of why the meeting is being called and a conviction that the work is worth doing. He ought to feel that his presence is necessary to the success of the gathering. He should share the facts on which other people at the meeting will be basing their thinking, and he needs a little time in advance to do some exploratory thinking on his own.

In the meeting he should feel that real work is underway

soon after the meeting begins. He ought to keep the group's task clearly in mind and always know how much is left to be done. He must understand what is being said and—to some degree—why. He must know when something has been decided—and what that something is. He needs to know why others voted as they did. He should learn new ideas or fresh slants from others and hope they will learn from him. He should come to like or respect the members as people more than ever.

After the meeting he should feel that he and others accomplished something worthwhile. He should recall some of the decisions with satisfaction and he should feel that the way was sound even though, to him, disappointing decisions were reached. He ought to feel that the meeting would not have been quite as good had he stayed home.

The program we offer recognizes the need of—and provides opportunities for—satisfying experiences for the members and concrete and important accomplishments for the board as a whole.

SCHEDULING THE BOARD MEETING

A school year is a year interlaced with deadlines. The next deadline is usually set so close to the last that there is little space between them. A board must thread its way among these deadlines, taking care not to trip and cause a legal tangle.

Custom and necessity set up a whole series of dates falling throughout the year for budgeting, bidding, opening and closing the fiscal period, meeting with the public, and holding elections. Likewise, there are deadlines for financial reporting, statistical reporting, applying for state and federal aid programs, inspections, and auditing local accounts.

The board adds, as needed, dates for meetings, adopting salary guides, paying bills, and visiting schools. The staff needs predictable, prompt board action on appointing personnel, setting salaries, granting tenure, approving leaves of absence, granting student awards, and issuing newsletters to the community.

Other deadlines arise from specific local circumstances: the home and school association invites the board to appear at a major public meeting next spring; a citizens' committee is asked to report in six months; the boards of education in a state or diocese schedule their annual conventions for the fall; or representatives of parents' groups ask to meet with the board before budgeting gets underway. If a building program is going on, it, too, contributes a rash of deadlines.

Happily, in one sense, many of these matters will reappear on the horizon next year at about the same spot they appeared this year. Thus they can be anticipated and provided for.

The superintendent or principal and the board secretary should keep a schedule of the board's known obligations for the entire calendar year ahead. Additional duties should be entered on the schedule as they arise from month to month. The list will help both board and staff see that nothing is left undone and that everything is done on time.

One good way to start such a master calendar is to scan board minutes for the past two or three years and draw out a list of recurring items, showing the dates on which they were considered. Entering these items on the calendar will be at least a beginning. Then continue by keeping a complete record carefully for one year. The result will be an excellent basis for laying out a master calendar for the following year.

As the year rolls by, the administrator and the board secretary should transfer specific items from the master calendar of board duties to the agenda of coming meetings. They should remind those persons who are responsible for preparing the necessary data or recommendations, and they should check again, several days in advance of each meeting, to see that everything required is ready to go to the board.

From time to time the board secretary should issue for all board members the exact schedule of meetings for the month or two ahead, listing new items of business as well as those recurring matters that have been drawn from the master calendar. This will stimulate the board and the staff to look ahead, perhaps to add some topics, to drop others, or to shift some to different meetings.

To schedule its own activities properly, the staff must develop the skill of planning backward from a known deadline to a necessary starting point. The master calendar of board duties, properly kept, can be of enormous help to the administrator, the secretary, and others who prepare materials and recommendations for the board. It can help them make up their own master calendar of "when to get started" on the various jobs they have to perform.

THE BOARD MEMBER'S HOMEWORK

The success of the meeting depends not only upon what people do while they are sitting and talking but also—and perhaps to an even greater degree—upon what has been done before they begin to talk and upon what will be done after they finish.

The work of a board meeting should be half finished before the chairman calls the group to order. In advance of the meeting, members should have received a folder containing copies of the agenda, an administrative staff memorandum suggesting a specific action (and even the exact wording of recommended resolutions) on agenda items, and any necessary supporting documents providing the facts and arguments on which the administration's recommendation is based. In addition, the folder should contain other enclosures such as routine reports and materials that the administration is passing on to the board for information only. Before the meeting begins, board members should have studied this material. They should know the questions they want to ask, and have a fairly good idea of how they want to vote .

Board members need time to do all this homework. Major reports, or those running more than a few pages, ought to be mailed as soon as they become available. Routine material can be collected, organized in the folder, and mailed so that members get it at least *two or three days ahead.* Each board member should receive a separate folder of material for each meeting—the folder dated—and this should be saved, with the minutes of that meeting slipped into it after they are written and approved, for future reference.

A board member ought to devote two or three hours to reading and thinking about the contents of his folder in preparation for the coming meeting. The man who cannot spare this much time is too busy for board membership.

He should begin by scanning the agenda to see the scope of the meeting, and should be sure to note on the folder flap any shifts he thinks would be desirable in the agenda format. Then he should dig into the administrative staff memorandum, stopping to examine relevant supporting documents as he goes. On the action items, he should study the material until he is sure he has all the data he needs to convince himself whether the action is desirable. Where he finds gaps of fact or significant opinions missing, he should jot questions on the folder flap so that they will spring immediately to mind when he opens his folder on meeting night. If time allows, he can call the administrator in advance and tell him the questions he wants answered before he will feel ready to vote. This step is especially needed when the administrator would not have the answer at his fingertips in the meeting and would need time beforehand for investigation.

When the folder contains administrative reports and informative materials that do not call for immediate action, the board member should note questions he wants to ask, points he wants to discuss, additional information he needs, and the date he would like to see the matters presented for action. He should also note on the folder flap the questions raised with him by citizens if he wishes to discuss these with the board or with the administrative staff.

The materials recommended for inclusion in the folder —the agenda, the administrative memorandum, and the supporting documents and other enclosures—will answer, as he studies them, the three questions a board member asks about every meeting.

The first question is, "What are we supposed to talk about tonight?"

THE AGENDA

Getting ready for a board meeting takes planning and coordinated effort. The quantity of that effort, however, is not nearly so important as its quality. Five minutes to decide whether a subject is ready for board study can save fifty minutes in a meeting. Ten minutes to draft the right paragraph will succeed where ten days to grind out the wrong report will fail.

The agenda for each meeting should be prepared in the administrator's office, either by the administrator or by the board's secretary working jointly with him. When necessary, either one can telephone the board chairman for advice.

All items headed for the board, regardless of their source, should come through the administrator's office whenever possible. There are two major reasons for this, both having to do with the two major functions the administrator performs directly for the board. The first of these functions is that of acting as executive officer for the board in carrying out its previously made policy decisions. This means that the administrator should be screening the various letters, requests, petitions, that individuals and groups are sending to the board—many of which will require only administrative disposition and can be handled by the administrator in line with established board policy.

The second major type of direct help the administrator gives the board is the preparation of material in a form suitable for the board's consideration. To make ready for board study and action those business items that he cannot handle directly himself, the administrator may need to clarify the wishes of the person addressing the board, make copies of that person's request or proposal, add information, attach his own comments about the effect or desirability of the proposed action, and offer his own recommendation about what steps the board should take.

The deadline for all agenda items should fall on the day before the meeting material is to be mailed to board members. This is not done as a bow to routine, but because things arriving any later cannot be processed for advance mailing. And advance mailing is essential. Jamming late items into the hopper can almost be guaranteed to monkey-wrench the operating machinery. Littering the board table with fresh material at meeting time diverts time from scheduled business, and slights these new items (which probably will be postponed after some stumbling discussion anyway). Worst of all, this builds bad habits into board, public, and staff alike.

Yes, but what about the authentic, full-fledged emergency that does sometimes develop after material has been mailed but before the meeting is called to order? Here's what to do: imagine that the situation had developed one day *after* the meeting. What would you have done in that case:

—Handled it administratively? Then do that now.

—Postponed it until the next meeting? Then do that.

—Called a special board meeting? Then do so.

If it means calling a special meeting, perhaps your board will be lucky and its regular meeting will adjourn early enough for a special session before normal adjournment time. If not, the board will have to choose another evening.

Beforehand, the agenda sheet outlines the evening's work. During, it lets the board member look ahead, helps him keep track, shows how the board is doing, tells it when to stop talking and move on. Afterward, it indexes what has been discussed at the meeting, guides him to the particular memo or enclosure he is trying to dig out of his old folders. The minutes, as everyone has learned by now, never tell the whole story and he will need the supplementary information that comes with the meeting material in order to engage in worthwhile future research. But if he has followed the procedures suggested above—filed the minutes of a meeting in the folder for that meeting—his research will be fruitful. He will have in one place a record of what was *discussed,* what was *recommended,* the facts behind the recommendations, and what was *decided.*

The chairman should know the shape of the whole meeting and keep its image before the board, the staff, and the audience. Thus, he should be thoroughly familiar with the entire agenda. He has other work, too: focusing on main issues; exploring the consequences of various choices; encouraging pointed discussion; helping members to understand exactly where they disagree; building agreement wherever possible; and winding up the conversation when it starts going around instead of ahead.

He should move down the agenda in order, ordinarily calling for a motion on each *action* item before opening a discussion on it. He will, of course, not call for such motions when no action has been recommended. When the talk gets hung on a snag and needs a flood of facts to float it off, the chairman should push the matter to the bottom of the agenda, or let it lay over until the next meeting, if possible. More often than not, he will want to refer it to the staff for additional facts or a fresh recommendation that the board might be willing to accept. When the chairman senses that nothing can happen to an item that night, then the sooner he acts to move the meeting forward, the better. Well-run meetings should see all action items completed in about one hour.

Classic board agenda organization is rarely questioned. Virtually everything ever written about the regular business meeting agenda suggests a pattern roughly like the following:

1. Opening of meeting
2. Approval of minutes
3. Communications
4. Hearing of delegations
5. Committee reports
6. Administrator's report
7. Old business
8. New business
9. Adjournment

The relationship of administrators to boards has changed enormously since such an agenda organization first became common. Moreover, we have learned a great deal in recent

years about the way people behave in meetings and about
what makes meetings productive and satisfying, or ineffective
and frustrating. The agenda format we recommend—as shown
below—takes the professional role of the chief administrator, plus individual and group psychology into account. It
probably looks like nothing you have come across before.
With practice in using it, you should be able to get results in
your meetings unlike anything you have experienced previously.

BUSINESS MEETING AGENDA

A. Call to order

B. Recommended actions

    1. Routine matters

        a. Approval of minutes

        b. Approval of treasurer's report

    2. Old business

    3. New business

C. Information and proposals

    1. From delegations

    2. From nonstaff communications and reports

    3. From the administrator and staff

    4. From questions asked of, and by, board members

D. Future business

    1. Meeting dates

    2. Preview of topics for future agendas

    3. General discussion to guide future recommendations

E. Adjournment

Now let's put a microscope on this agenda.

Recommended actions. The fastest single way to clear away conversational underbrush at a board meeting is to draw a hard line between "action" and "no action" items. Almost everywhere there is a board which, after wrangling about something for half an hour, has finally turned to the administrator to ask in exasperation, "What do you want *us* to do about this?" and has been told, "Nothing. This is just for your information." This agenda format faces this problem squarely, breaks sharply with existing patterns to place *all* action items where they belong—together at the beginning.

First come the brief, familiar routines like standard monthly reports. Next are matters left over from previous meetings. Finally, the board takes up new topics on which action is being recommended for the first time. This done, all official board *action* is completed. Long before eyelids droop and heads nod, the board's decisions are firmly settled for the evening. No more ripening discussions chopped off to get a needed vote on $17.50 of overtime pay for the school custodian. No more bleary-eyed voting to regret the next day.

Information and proposals. This is a varied selection of matters from several different sources. None of the subjects has reached the stage where the administrative staff is ready to recommend definite action. They may be old or new topics. Often they will be matters of information requested by the board at some prior sessions. Just as often, the subject will be utterly new.

Information and proposals from delegations get first place on the bill because the board probably will not want to ask official visitors to wait too long for its attention.

Our agenda outline is based on the firm conviction that the public pulse is still beating at 9 p.m. It can be felt, and the public brow stroked, if necessary, at that time. By then the board will have completed all its *action* items for the evening, members will have a sense of firm accomplishment, and the time pressure and the attendant psychological pressure will be off. The situation, as well as the mood, will be better for dealing with delegations. And, just in case the session degenerates into a spontaneous display of oratory, no significant action item will be left hanging fire.

Following the delegations are all other communications and reports that do not come from the educational system. Correspondence, printed reports from outside organizations, and written reports from citizens' committees or community groups appear on the agenda list at this point. Reports from standing committees, if any such committees exist, would fall here. The chances are good that this will turn out to be a general catchall for the information and proposals that do not fit elsewhere.

The section held open for the administrator and staff is for the many "no action" matters they will present. It is *not* for the classic administrator's report, which customarily contained all his remarks to the board. That device was suitable enough in its day when the board handled finance, buildings, and community affairs directly and turned the spotlight on the administrator only briefly to hear a report on "instruction." But it is not suitable today when the administrator acts as executive officer for the board in its entire range of operations. He is involved in every aspect of board activity and consequently in every aspect of board meetings. Not that the administrator should dominate board meetings. He decidedly should not. What he in all likelihood will dominate, however, is the great variety of outside activities that precede and follow every meeting.

The next section of the agenda gives board members a definite opportunity to question the staff concerning various matters not listed for the meeting. Such questions come from citizens, from board members' own interests, from past agenda items, or from trains of thought started by the current agenda.

Future business. So much has to be accomplished by board and administrator in so little time, that planning by both is essential. Planning for the next meeting, in fact, is an essential part of the current meeting. The planning period comes at the *end* both for reasons of meeting structure and for reasons of group psychology. The staff and board can:

1. Review suggestions and decisions made earlier in the meeting concerning the inclusion and timing of future business.

2. Reserve meeting dates in light of these decisions and in light of other anticipated business.

3. Discuss these coming problems in order to guide the administrator in recommending action to the board.

4. End the meeting on the upswing with a stimulating look at the work ahead and a high-level discussion of how the board will approach it.

THE ADMINISTRATIVE STAFF MEMORANDUM

The second question board members ask about every meeting is, "What do the administrator and others think we should do about all this?"

The administrative staff memorandum, which should be included in the meeting folder supplied to each board member, contains staff reactions and recommendations. It tells the member exactly what the administrator thinks the board should do about each topic on the agenda. Of course, the board may act otherwise, but having the administrator's advice clearly set down will sharpen the issues, predetermine certain motions, and nearly always speed action in meetings.

Even when an item originates outside the administrative staff, the staff will still need to lay its reactions on top of these outside proposals. It may also have to support them with data about what the consequences of these proposals would be if they were adopted. Persons not on the administrative staff have no responsibility to point out all such implications.

Note that when the topic originates with the administrative staff, the actual *recommendations for action* should be separated from the background information that sets the stage for these recommendations. The background information, which in some cases will be long and detailed, should be part of the supporting material included in the folder.

The board should not be left to grope for words when it is time for action. The administrative staff memorandum should *state recommendations in language that can be incorporated into motions.*

Staff memoranda should be composed as each agenda item is selected in the weeks preceding the meeting. These memoranda can be collected and organized into a single document before being typed and duplicated—or they can be typed and duplicated separately.

In parishes and small systems the principal or superintendent will write most of the staff memoranda himself. To lighten the load in larger systems, the commentary on each subject may be written by the administrator in charge of that facet of educational affairs. Such writing normally should represent the superintendent's viewpoint. If the two viewpoints differ and both are to go before the board, the superintendent will need to write his own. In that case, it probably will be best to incorporate the recommendations of the subordinate administrator in the enclosures so that they will be available for the board's attention, but will not be confused with the superintendent's differing recommendations.

The administration should be sure to indicate in the administrative staff memorandum any items that are supplemented by the supporting documents, so that board members can refer to them at just the moment they are pertinent.

Administrative follow-up begins the moment a motion is passed and may go on for months before all the ends are securely tied. The staff should remain alert in meetings to all the consequences that will flow from each board action. During the meeting, the administrator should check off each approved item on the administrative staff memorandum and note on the folder flaps any special instructions to the staff.

Flipping open the folder the next morning, the administrator has the complete record before him—an organized guide for dictating letters, scheduling conferences, and instructing the staff to take the authorized actions. Any of his assistants who attended the meeting get the same kind of aid in planning their own follow-up activities.

THE SUPPORTING DOCUMENTS

The third question asked by board members at every meeting is, "What makes the staff think we ought to take the action it is recommending?"

The supporting documents and other enclosures are keyed in, at hand, ready to back up every recommendation and stack solid facts under the framework of every discussion. They tell almost everything the board needs to know before the meeting, are admirable conversation shorteners in the meeting itself, and last for years as history many people will want to read again.

Detailed reports of every description go to the board. Some go regularly, others go once for a single purpose. Some are only for information, others are to pave the road for action. Some are verbal, others are statistical, and still others are statistical with verbal interpretations. They may be prepared by:

Superintendent (Principal)	Government officials
Other administrators	Community groups
Staff committees	Citizens' committees
Board committees	Research agencies
Teachers' association	Commercial organizations
Students	Interested individuals
Parents' groups	Publications:
Employed consultants	Magazines
Diocesan offices	Newspapers
Pastor (s)	Newsletters
Bishop	Special reports

They flow into every board office in a heavy stream. Shunting some aside, diverting more into administrative channels, and filtering the remainder for the board's attention is a steady job for the administrator. He will need to make explanations when the enclosures relate to action items or specific proposals, but will often send them to the board without interpretation when they are simply for the board's general information. Long reports sent to the board a month or so ahead of their appearance in the recommended action section of a meeting can be drawn out of the old board meeting folders when they reappear on later agendas.

The supporting documents and other enclosures fall into two broad categories: those originating within the system, such as reports from principals, department heads, the chief custodian, the board clerk, and the treasurer; and those originating outside the system such as reports, letters, and requests from government agencies, community committees and organizations, and individual citizens. They should be prepared in the weeks preceding the meeting. Comments concerning them may be written for the administrative staff memorandum as each enclosure is prepared. Enclosures need not be prepared in the administrator's office, but can be typed and duplicated elsewhere. Delegating the typing and duplicating to other secretarial personnel keeps the clerical burden of preparing for board meetings better distributed.

Priority goes to the reports and requests that provide background for recommended actions. They must be included with the meeting material in every case. Next in importance come those that inform the board about the operation of its policies, then those that need action in coming weeks, and finally, those that improve the board's overall understanding of education and of its own functions. If time is running out and some reports cannot be finished soon enough for the meeting, the administration should work on them in the above order and postpone the leftover matters until the next meeting.

Regular use of well-organized folders containing materials such as we've described will bring ease and simplicity to the writing of board meeting minutes. The secretary, equipped in advance with a complete board meeting information folder, should be familiar with the topics to be considered, the action recommended by the administrative staff, and the wording of any pre-written motions. During the meeting, the secretary should follow the board's action closely, initialing as approved any present motions, writing out new motions, and collecting for official signatures those schedules and other documents approved during the meeting. The secretary should ask the designated board signatories to sign such documents at the close of the meeting. After the meeting, the secretary should record, in the form favored by the board, the disposition of all items on which action was recommended, all motions passed by the board, and all important instructions given to the staff. Approved schedules should be referred to by number, title, and date in the body of the minutes and included in the official minute book as part of the record.

PUBLIC PARTICIPATION IN MEETINGS

In addition to board members, the meetings should be attended by the administrator, his assistants when they will be of help, the board's secretary, the treasurer or the counsel when appropriate, and the person assigned to draft board policies.

A board does not meet chiefly to hear the public. The public attends to hear the board. Keep that clear. But it is true that controlled public participation can help the board understand the wishes of the people and help the people understand the board and education.

The audience should contain, in addition to interested members of the public, representatives of local newspapers if they are available to cover school news, or the staff writer of school publicity if they are not.

At various times, representatives of other diocesan or parish bodies, citizens' committees, staff committees, parent groups, students, individual teachers, principals (in the case of diocesan boards), and individual members of the public may be invited to report to the board orally.

In this board meeting format as we have outlined it, board members study written information at home in advance. Consequently, the audience loses the chance to hear the staff report this information during meetings. What the audience gets in exchange is an infinitely more valuable opportunity to hear their representatives mull over issues, discuss the facts, try out tentative ideas, state viewpoints, suggest solutions, and work out decisions. They witness action rather than details. *This* is the sort of talk that is really worth listening to at a board meeting.

Place extra copies of the evening's agenda by the door so that people who come to observe can pick them up as they enter. Although the administrative staff memorandum will often contain confidential remarks, you will probably find that for some meetings at least, it will be possible and desirable to make copies of that memorandum available to the public. More frequently, spare copies of selected non-confidential enclosures will be of interest to the audience. Such enclosures should be distributed whenever possible.

There are two customary ways for the public to take part in open board sessions. The first is for one or more persons to address the board concerning some matter on which they wish it to take action. The agenda reserves a place for hearing such delegations. They should be scheduled for that spot and limited to it unless there are unusual reasons for hearing them elsewhere.

The second way is for the audience to ask questions and to offer comments. Judicious control by the board may be needed to hold this practice within sensible bounds. Sometimes the audience gets thoroughly entangled in the discussion and does not want to be cut out.

No matter when questions arise, board members should not feel obligated to argue with the public about their own voting or other actions. The people are, of course, entitled to an explanation of the policies the board is following in making this or that decision, but the merits of particular cases and the soundness of individual members' opinions are not up for public debate.

If you want good coverage, news of board meetings should go to the newspapers immediately following the sessions. By definition, "old news" is not "news."

Dailies will need to get stories during or at the end of meetings if the material is to be worth their paper and ink.

Whenever possible, try to release information to newspaper reporters in advance. Foreknowledge of meeting content helps reporters plan their stories and gives them time to ask their editors to reserve adequate space.

Weeklies move at a slower pace and can use news write-ups even two or three days after the events occur. But here, too, the sooner the write-up is turned in, the better your chance of getting the full story printed in a visible location.

If reporters attend your meetings, they will find the written agenda of value in following board action. The administrative staff memorandum is even more valuable. Its short summaries of reasons for recommendations and its pre-written motions are the finest kind of help a reporter can have in writing his stories. They almost do the job for him, even to giving him brief, accurate quotations. Sometimes a commentary will contain confidential information that you may not wish to give to reporters. It may still be possible to provide them with those sections that are not confidential. Some school systems have developed such sound relations with the press that reporters are given the complete memorandum with confidential material clearly marked on the press copies. Reporters scrupulously omit from their stories all such confidential information in return for the benefits of using the rest of the memorandum. Each board and administrator will, of course, act as the local situation demands.

Selected enclosures—or all of them if the press is interested enough—can go to reporters either for their own background information, or for summarizing in print, or even for reproducing in full when appropriate.

If reporters do not cover your board meetings, someone will have to prepare publicity releases for the papers if you want to appear in print. The choice of writers is wide. Perhaps the administrator himself will have to do the job in small systems and parishes. In larger systems he probably will select some member of the administrative staff, a teacher who can attend board meetings, a competent clerk, the board secretary, or a willing citizen with a talent for writing. Members of the board should not be burdened with this job.

The system's periodic newsletter, if any such exists, or an occasional bulletin can carry the board's complete story to the public better than most other media. Here the emphasis will probably not be on reporting individual meetings, but rather on describing the board's broad purposes and its overall educational program.

VIII

How the Board Can Assess
Educational Outcomes

WHAT THE BOARD CAN'T DO

One of the board's key tasks is to determine whether the educational program of the diocese or parish is accomplishing what it is supposed to accomplish. To do that the board first must set some clearly stated and understood goals for student achievement. Then it must look for evidence that what is going on in the educational program is enabling students to reach those goals.

A "good" educational program is one that can demonstrate to a board's satisfaction that goals are being reached. Note the emphasis here. Student achievement is the one and only criterion. *All other matters*—beauty of buildings, pupil/ teacher ratio, length of school day, public relations program, teacher salaries—*are secondary.* They are means to the end of student achievement. That is not to say that they are unimportant. It is to say that questions of the "best" buildings, loads, salaries, and so on can only be judged in relation to their effectiveness in promoting educational output—that is, student achievement.

In weighing educational outcomes, the board cannot monitor the processes of education. It cannot, and should not try to, direct the professional staff in *how* to teach, maintain discipline, or create courses of study, for example. The *how* of education is the domain of the professional educator. Nothing but harm can come from a board's delving into that area because laymen, to put it bluntly, are ignorant of what today's good teaching encompasses.

The medical profession, for example, has gone so far along the route of technical and scientific development that no lay hospital board of trustees can possibly pass upon procedures for patient care, upon the relative merits of one anesthetic over another, upon the question of whether a given piece of tissue should or should not be removed by surgery.

Larger and larger parcels of authority, power, and expectancy for self-discipline have been vested in the medical professional because laymen simply do not have the knowledge and the technical competence to understand and make judgments. The medical staff of the hospital must even play a major role in the selection of its own members. How can a layman pass judgment on the competence of an internist? A cardiac specialist? A brain surgeon?

We can see the same dilemma at the university level in education. Can a board of trustees of a university, or the president, make intelligent judgments about courses of study in celestial mechanics, cultural anthropology, or medieval literature?

Of course they cannot. They rely upon the specialized knowledge of department heads and individual faculty members. There is a fundamental difference between the legal power[1] of the board and the inherent power of specialization in the faculty:

Legal power grows out of the responsibility of governing boards to the larger community and their positions as custodians of their institutions. They delegate this power to executives and administrative staffs for the executive direction of schools, colleges, and universities, and, frequently, to faculties for the approval of educational programs.

---

[1]By "legal" is meant the authority of the board under Church and civil law. See Chapter II.

Inherent power rests upon the experience, talents, and occupational genius employed in the pursuit and propagation of knowledge.

> Faculties monopolize the necessary understanding of the subject matter and contacts with others in the 'field' and thus make the decisions which shape the academic functions of their institutions. This knowledge, with subsequent initiative in proposing new faculty members, curricular changes, and similar matters, blunts the force of executive authority from boards.[2]

The conflict between the two kinds of power is more serious, thus far, at the university level than at the secondary and elementary levels. But the time is approaching when local boards of education will be saying, as in this "Paley Report" on *The Role of the Trustees of Columbia University:*

> How can trustees carry out their public responsibility of supervising their institutions when they are substantially or almost completely separated from the paramount function of their organization, its educational program?[3]

How can *you* board members carry out your public responsibility as you become less and less knowledgeable about the technical aspects of the educational program? Will you have to abdicate, as is practically now the case with hospital trustees, to the professional staff?

We offer as a guide to understanding a "loop concept" developed by Henry M. Brickell and Daniel R. Davies.[4] It logically relates *objectives* to *action* by way of the decision making process, and then shows how the resulting action can be reported back and evaluated in relation to objectives through *process.*

[2]*Management of Learning,* New Dimensions in Higher Education, No. 5, U.S. Department of Health, Education and Welfare, Office of Education, 1960, p. 19.

[3]*Ibid.,* p. 16.

[4]Davies, Daniel R., and Brickell, Henry M., "The Board and the Curriculum," *School Board Policies,* March, 1963.

PROCESS AND PRODUCT REPORTS

Start by assuming that somewhere, someplace, there is a set of *objectives* for the system. Think of them as the kind of objectives that parents and other members of the community have for their children. Then, both theory and practice say that the board of education adopts *policies* indicating the general directions and limits of discretion to be enjoyed by the professional staff in its work. Thus far, then, the loop looks like this:

The administrative staff then makes *regulations* spelling out in detail how the policies of the board are to be carried out. The regulations lead to *action*. The loop now looks like this:

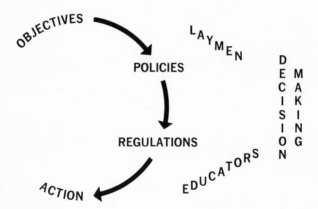

The right side of the loop shows the familiar process whereby the board of education makes decisions (policies) in the light of wishes (objectives) that the people of the community (laymen) have for their programs of education. The administration then makes decisions (regulations) to translate the board's policy decisions into educational programs (action).

If you stop at that point, something important is missing. How is the board to know how effective the action is? The board needs a systematic, regular flow of information to enable it to make judgments about what is happening.

Start up the left side of the loop. The first kind of information the board gets is in *process reports:*

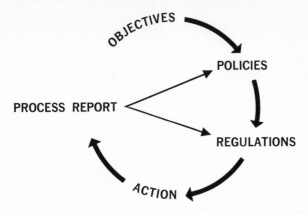

Most of the reports given to boards are process reports. They tell, for example, class size, pupil/teacher ratio, educational level of the teaching staff, financial data. They shed practically no light on whether the system is achieving its objectives.

The second kind of information given to boards is contained in *product reports.* These describe the output of the educational program—reporting, for example, on scores on standardized achievement tests, per cent of pupils who stay in school till graduation, per cent of graduates placed in jobs or in colleges of their choice. The loop is now complete.

The left side of the loop points out the two kinds of reports that will enable the board to fulfill its monitoring function: process and product reports. We maintain that a lay board *can* monitor the performance of a professional staff given *three key conditions:*

1. That the board starts with a clear statement of objectives understandable to laymen.

2. That the board adopts and maintains a written set of policies designed to set the conditions most likely to achieve the objectives.

3. That the board insists on a good set of both process *and* product reports. The latter are especially important because they enable the board to close the loop by comparing *results* with the stated *objectives.*

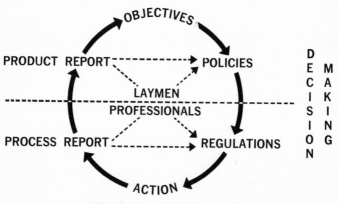

THE DAVIES–BRICKELL LOOP

Notice in the completed loop that the work of the laymen of the board and of the community is primarily above the hemisphere line, and that the work of the professional is mainly below it.

Let us see how the loop might work in practice. A board of education receives an annual report of results stemming from the *stated objective,* "All students who could profit from further education enter post-high school institutions." They start at the top of the loop with a clean-cut statement in laymen's language. Next. . .

The board adopted a set of policies:

1. The high schools shall have varied curricula.

2. The high schools shall have comprehensive testing

programs.

3.   The high schools shall have comprehensive guidance services.

The staff prepared a set of administrative regulations designed to implement the policies. These dealt with:

1.   Courses offered.
2.   Tests scheduled.
3.   Counselors' load, etc.

The administrator made a series of process reports:

1.   Enrollment figures in curricula and courses.
2.   Number of tests administered.
3.   Test results. (Note that these are process in relation to the stated objective!)
4.   Statistics on load.

Finally came the product report. It was built around the percentage of graduates following each of several careers and the ability levels of students as high, medium, or low:

Graduates Entering	Ability	%
4-Year Colleges	H-M	60
2-Year Colleges	H-M-L	15
Commercial Schools	M-L	15
Military Service	H-M-L	5
Marriage	M-L	3
Work	L	2

The board then had the actual *product* data directly related to the original objective.

The effects of the findings? The board felt rather comfortable about the school's performance. High and medium ability students *were* seeking further training in very satisfactory percentages. The board members asked themselves, though, whether the schools might do more for those few going directly into marriage and work. In the case of this particular community, the problem was definitely a minor one, according to the product *evidence*.

You now know a route by which a board can evaluate the total educational program. To do so, the board needs, first a set of objectives stated in laymen's language. Second, it needs a set of written policies consistent with those objectives. Third, it supports the administrative staff in its development of regulations to bring about action. Fourth, it receives both process and product reports, with emphasis upon the latter. The product reports especially shed light upon the effectiveness of the system in achieving the people's objectives.

Superintendents of education should encourage administrators of educational units to create an atmosphere of professional equality within their respective administrative, instructional, clerical and custodial staffs. They can do this by reducing authority levels, practicing honest cooperative planning, and emphasizing nonmaterial rewards.

Create a "predictable environment" for employees through written board policies and administrative regulations available to each board member, each administrator, each teacher, and each other employee. One study[5] shows that teachers feel a greater sense of security in some large school systems than in small ones. The explanation advanced is that in those larger school systems, written systems of policies existed, whereas in the small school systems, there were none. Employees prefer having access to "ground rules" that have been cooperatively developed and are in writing, to having to trust memory, whims, and favors of any one administrator or board, no matter how able, when a problem arises.

To deal intelligently and adequately with the problems arising out of the pushing of complex subject matter further and further down into our secondary and elementary grades, and growing out of the increasing technology of teaching:

. . .Keep clearly in mind that difference between a layman's problem (upper hemisphere of the loop) and a professional's problem (lower hemisphere).

. . .Focus on *lay objectives* for education. Work with your superintendent and his staff in developing and adopting policies that point out your *general intent.* Then let the pro-

---

[5]Moellet, Gerald H., "Teaching Perceptions of Administrative Behavior," study jointly reported by Washington University, St. Louis, and the U.S. Office of Education, 1962.

fessional staff take over on procedures and processes. Staff pride and feelings of responsibility cannot fail to go up when a board says, in effect, "Here is what we'd like to see accomplished. We know what we want, but we don't know how to get it because we don't have the professional training. We authorize you to work out the procedures in the light of your training and experience. We trust you."

. . .Seek the development of *product measures* related to *objectives* to guide policy development and to enable you to estimate the effectiveness of your programs. Emphasize outcomes and leave processes to the professionals. Base your appeals for financial support on results, on products— *not* upon processes alone.

IX

Catholic Education:
Its Purposes and Problems

GOALS: PAST, PRESENT, AND FUTURE

The aim of this book is to help Catholic boards of education do their work, not dictate to them the goals they should pursue or the policies they should adopt. Nevertheless, no treatment of Catholic education would be complete without an examination of its broad objectives, both those sought in the past and those proposed today by many leading educators in response to new conditions in the Catholic Church and American society. Admittedly, much of what follows is subject to controversy; it cannot, however, be ignored by any board of education alert to contemporary challenges.

The widespread implementation of the Baltimore Council's decrees on the establishment of Catholic schools does not mean that that legislation met with universal approval. There was resistance, and it arose not simply from financial or staffing problems but from philosophical concerns as well.

The desire of second-generation Catholic Americans to fit in with American cultural patterns was generally supported by most Catholic bishops in the latter half of the nineteenth century. In 1890 Archbishop John Ireland of St. Paul, Minn., attempted to arrange a marriage between the public schools and Catholic desire for in-school religious instruction. Like most marriages, this one depended on the willingness of both parties to accept substantial compromises. Ireland's plan called for Catholic children to enroll in publicly controlled and operated schools in which religion could be taught outside regular school hours. Some influential and conservative Churchmen, however, viewed it as a dangerous watering-down of Catholic educational requirements. Similar plans have usually proven equally unacceptable to many public school policy makers. These latter have rather consistently condemned such proposals on grounds that they run counter to the "melting pot" process, foster "divisiveness" among children along religious and ethnic lines by recognizing their differing loyalties and origins, and are of dubious legal stature under the First Amendment.

Parochial schools became a means of preserving religious loyalty, and were established more in reaction to the prevailing public philosophy and the intense anti-Catholicism then found in public schools than from a freely-chosen, positive desire for separate education. Indeed, most nineteenth century bishops were ahead of their flocks in resisting the urge to transfer bitter ethnic and religious quarrels to the New World. Few of the predominantly Irish hierarchy were very sympathetic to the "national churches," which grouped immigrant Catholics into parishes homogeneous in language, customs, and style of worship. If Catholic schools are sometimes accused of helping form Catholic "ghettos," it should be clear that these, like the enclaves of Jews in the Middle Ages, were much more imposed upon than chosen by Catholic leaders.

This goal of encouraging loyalty to the Church arose, then, out of the nature of nineteenth century American culture. The manner of meeting the need was suited to the times and to the schools' constituency and proved remarkably effective. Catholic schools did preserve the faith for second and successive generations while showing genius in generally assisting, rather than hindering, the Americanization process. In a landmark study of Catholic school influence *(The Education of Catholic Americans.* Chicago: 1966) Andrew Greeley and Peter Rossi showed the remarkably positive influence on religious behavior induced by sustained Catholic school attendance. Catholic schools, therefore, were a highly successful response to the first law of life for institutions as for individuals—that is, survival.

In the century since the Council of Baltimore, American Catholicism has changed radically, as has the larger society in which American Catholics live. Today Catholic Americans are, typically, neither immigrants nor the children of immigrants. They perceive relatively little tension between their Church membership and the goals of American society.

Especially since Vatican II, the American Catholic Church has been reexamining its own institutional goals. Clearly, survival will always be fundamental. But few leaders of the Church today question its ability to survive in the American environment, albeit in much changed form. Once survival is fairly assured, the organization, like the individual, can ask the question: survival for what? The revision of Church and church-school goals starts from the same point, response to the larger cultural environment. The most pertinent question being asked of Catholic schools today is not *can* they survive, but *should* they survive—are they needed in America today?

It is ironic that in a society whose needs are dramatically, even traumatically, called to our attention daily, this question can ever be posed. Both the institutional Church and the civil society need these schools as never before. It is quite clear that Vatican II turned the Catholic Church outward, causing it increasingly to identify its own aims with society's. The two major encyclicals of Pope John XXIII, *Mater et Magistra* and *Pacem in Terris,* dwelt almost exclusively on social concerns, and a recent papal letter by Pope Paul VI, *The Progress of Peoples,* even caused speculation in conservative circles that the Pope was strongly influenced by communism! These papal statements are both signs and causes of a growing tendency to expand the concept of the Church in such a way that "what is good for society is good for religion" begins to assume the character of doctrine.

If this tendency to equate ecclesiastical and social needs is correctly described, certain conclusions follow for today's Catholic schools.

> Among pupils of different talents and backgrounds it [the school] promotes friendly relations and fosters a spirit of mutual understanding, and it establishes, as it were, a center whose work and progress must be shared together by families, teachers, and associations of various types that foster cultural, civic, and religious life, as well as by civil society and the entire human community.[1]

Elsewhere this *Declaration on Christian Education* states that the Church is interested in education not only in order to further the salvation of souls, but also "for the good of earthly society and for the building of a better world."

The continuing translation of this post-Vatican II view of the Church's role into the educational apostolate is seen in the 1968 statement of the Washington Symposium on Catholic Education:

> Catholic thinking on education increasingly recognizes that the most significant educational goals are best achieved in an atmosphere of freedom. Among these goals the Catholic approach places great emphasis on development of intellectual competence, on the achievement of an ordered understanding of human and revealed truth, on the awakening of creative powers and cultural awareness....It [Catholic education] seeks therefore to foster personal charity and generosity, an overriding commitment to social justice at every level of the human community, political maturity, respect for the sacredness of man, a practiced sensitivity toward ethical criteria in professional, business and family life.[2]

We may then draw a few conclusions that offer very general guidelines to those attempting to formulate goals for Catholic schools:

[1]*Declaration on Christian Education* in Abbott, W.M., S.J., ed., *The Documents of Vatican II* (New York, 1966), p. 643.

[2]*Catholic Education Today and Tomorrow* (Washington, 1968), pp. 113-114.

1. No goals may be considered static and immutable. The only objectives of Catholic education that can be termed unchangeable are those so enormously general that they offer little more guidance than "do good and avoid evil."

2. Many goals are related to, even identified with, the valid goals of human society. They are not only "Catholic," but rather "catholic" in application and purpose.

3. From the foregoing it seems that goals for Catholic schools might well be of two kinds: *personal goals,* based on the individual child's need for adequate physical care, recognition, acceptance and affection, and intellectual and cultural development in an atmosphere of maximum personal freedom; and *societal* or *community goals* based on the need for peace among nations, justice and charity among religious and ethnic groups, reduction of poverty and ignorance, and rational use of leisure time.

This book attempts simply to survey Catholic education while concentrating on that system's policy formation process. Obviously the above "goals" are depicted in the broadest strokes. Yet any attempt to spell out objectives in terms applicable to the enormous variety of Catholic educational systems and institutions goes far beyond the intent or possiblities of this work.

EDUCATIONAL PRIORITIES

The Church insists in Canon Law that its schools are public schools and cites as proof the fact that they perform a public function (Canon 1375). The United States Supreme Court has recognized this public service performed by nonpublic schools, and used it as a justification for spending public tax monies to support these public services. Furthermore, as noted above, the Catholic Church, especially since Vatican II, has tended increasingly to identify its own needs and interests with the legitimate desires of the society in which it lives.

This concept of service by the Church to society is certainly realized to some extent by any good Catholic school.

But recently prominent educators, sickened at the widespread failure of public education to reach and substantially improve the lives of inner-city children, have suggested a massive redirection of Catholic educational resources into the area of greatest need, the heart of our major cities. In a speech to the 1968 National Catholic Educational Association convention, U.S. Commissioner of Education Harold Howe II urged Catholic educators to stem the loss of educational resources from the inner-city and there direct the major thrust of their school efforts.

Just a month before Commissioner Howe's address, Monsignor James Donohue, director of the Department of Education of the United States Catholic Conference, urged in an article in *America* magazine that the Church review its priorities in education, placing enormously increased personnel and financial resources in the city ghettos and accepting the unavoidable consequence of a greatly reduced school presence in suburbia.

Such proposals—which are echoed by many concerned educators, Catholic and non-Catholic—suggest, when viewed against these troubled times, that new and urgent priorities must be established for Catholic education.

It is generally agreed that every Catholic of every age and economic condition has a right to Catholic education. This right must be translated into methods of education appropriate to various levels of age and understanding. The most suitable vehicle for formal education of young Catholics is a school offering high quality instruction in all areas of learning, preeminently religion, and with religious values pervading every aspect of its program.

Most Catholic parents want their children in this kind of school. The fulfillment of this desire should not be considered financially impossible by Catholic educational policy makers and administrators until they can honestly and accurately state that, although everything possible has been done to increase income, maximize operating efficiency, and make the best possible use of personnel resources, the difficulties remain insuperable.

If indeed it proves impossible to provide money and personnel for good school education at every level, then some painful decisions must be made:

1. Catholic schools should first serve those whose educational needs are greatest. It seems clear that the need for good secular education and good moral environment is most acute for children in our inner-city slums. Many ghetto public schools are unable to offer the kind of education students require. Children attending these schools frequently are denied the highly skilled assistance they need to learn basic educational skills. It is equally evident that neighborhood environment and home situations in the slums frequently work against the formation of strong moral values. Thus good quality religious school education seems most critically needed in the inner-city.

2. Catholic children in the outer-city and suburbs may not be "written off" by Church educators. True, these children usually have available to them public schools that provide adequate to excellent "secular" teaching. Usually the home, neighborhood, and school environments are capable of inculcating desirable moral values fairly effectively, especially in younger children. However, these influences will usually be incomplete without formal and systematic instruction in religion—reinforced by worship, social action, and adult-child contacts that will tend to inculcate Christian values.

In those metropolitan regions where heavy concentrations of money and teachers in poverty area schools will result in curtailment of some suburban schools, the diocese and parishes should focus attention on:

(a) Helping suburban parents develop desirable values and motives in their young children (infancy to age eight).

(b) Organizing Sunday and summer school programs that combine instruction with group task and play activities for children aged nine to 12.

(c) Cooperating with leaders of other faiths, and public school officials, in instituting courses about religion in public high schools.

(d) Working with these same groups in setting up released time programs in religion for high school students, conducted by professional teachers and, where possible, taken for credit.

(e) Where (c) and (d) prove impossible, establishing professionally-staffed catechetical centers for teenagers.

(f) Offering a variety of religious experiences and community welfare activities to teenagers and young adults.

The Church's educational effort in the ghetto must clearly be undertaken as an unselfish religious response to a desperate social need. In some areas the most effective means of help may be professional services donated to local public school systems. Where ghetto religious schools are maintained and strengthened, these could frequently be ecumenically controlled and staffed. In all cases, admission to religious schools operated in poverty areas should be on the basis of educational need, not of individual creed.

In areas where Catholic suburban and inner-city schools can both be maintained, there should be "pairing" of parishes or groups of parishes. This should facilitate not only financial assistance to the poorer parish, but pupil and teacher exchanges, donated services, and cooperation of students and faculty in community tasks. Centralization of financial and personnel resources and distribution of these on the basis of need are further recommended as means of improving school services to those most requiring help.

Careful planning should precede any notable change. Since changes are certainly ahead for Catholic schools, Catholic boards of education, in cooperation with religious communities, should undertake a thorough evaluation of current educational endeavors, goals and resources, and on the basis of such an evaluation plan commitments for the future.

All Catholic educators ought carefully to consider the following excerpt from the *Statement on National Race Crisis* issued on April 25, 1968, by the National Conference of Catholic Bishops:

> Education is a basic need in our society, yet the schooling available to the poor is pitifully inadequate. We cannot

break the vicious cycle of poverty producing poverty unless we achieve a breakthrough in our educational system. Quality education for the poor, and especially for minorities who are traditionally victims of discrimination, is a moral imperative if we are to give millions a realistic chance to achieve basic human dignity. Catholic school systems, at all levels, must redouble their efforts, in the face of changing social patterns and despite their own multiple problems, to meet the current social crisis. This crisis is of a magnitude and peril far transcending any which the Church in America or the nation has previously confronted.[3]

NEEDS AND PROBLEMS

Education today does not lack problems. One man's list of these is probably as good as another's. Here we shall group the difficulties of Catholic educational systems quite arbitrarily under two general headings: those that pose real obstacles to continued growth, and those that, conceivably, constitute great opportunities disguised as insoluble crises.

One could easily get the impression, especially from the more liberal Catholic press, that the American layman is straining at his clerically imposed leash. Many pastors and bishops have found to their sorrow that this is usually not the case. Possibly the most serious obstacle to improvement in Catholic education is the rather widespread reluctance of laymen—nonclerics and noneducators—to share in decision making. In the 1966 survey of diocesan boards, one-fifth of the board chairmen said they preferred that their boards possess advisory authority only, while nearly one-half preferred that their decisions be subject to review by the local bishop. When asked more specifically to check a list of functions, the board chairmen showed themselves even less anxious to assume substantial responsibility for policy decisions. In regard to none of the 28 listed functions did as many as two-thirds

[3]National Conference of Catholic Bishops, *Statement on National Race Crisis.*

of the chairmen feel they should properly be making decisions; on the other hand, superintendents of education in the same dioceses indicated, by more than two-thirds approval, their desire that the boards exercise authority in at least 15 of the listed areas. Only a handful of the superintendents indicated a desire that the boards' authority be limited to advice giving. Whatever the limitations of the survey, it hints at an unwillingness on the part of board chairmen to assume real responsibility for the educational system, while indicating that superintendents are generally willing to see such a transfer of authority.

A second obstacle that could blight the future of Catholic education is the continued insistence in some dioceses and parishes upon traditional structures of policy formation and administration. An overwhelming majority of dioceses and nearly half the parishes in the country with parochial schools now have boards of education. A few bishops and a more substantial number of pastors, however, cannot see the value—indeed the compelling necessity—for broadening the decision making process in Catholic education. This continued myopia can result in ever-growing handicaps for schools and school systems. There is, of course, no guarantee that improved policy making procedures will of themselves "save" Catholic education, but there are excellent reasons to believe that a monolithic, clerically dominated approach will guarantee its demise.

Although, as should be clear by now, the authors of this book are on the side of the board movement in Catholic education, they have tried to point out certain hazards that accompany the board process. Members of Catholic boards of education, like their public school counterparts, must be acutely aware of the dangers of parochialism (a hazard not confined to parishes). Education is becoming increasingly national and international in its scope. The cherished public school board ideal of local control, while it does preserve traditional and very real values, is nonetheless quite obviously creating increasing problems. Board members at every level of Catholic education must constantly be reminded of their responsibilities toward the diocese and the Church as a whole, as well as toward their local community and the citizens of their state, their nation, and the world community.

Another danger inherent in the nonprofessional's approach to education is an attempt to transfer procedures and philosophies directly from other professions. An educational system, public or nonpublic, is not "just like" a household, a medical practice, or a factory. And board members must recognize that methods and practices appropriate to the conduct of a profit-making business, for example, may well be inappropriate to the conduct of a school system. It is probably true, for instance, that the most efficient source of operating income for nonpublic schools is tuition. But if a board decrees that all or much of school income will be raised through charges levied directly on the pupil and his parents, the result may be contrary to the board's intentions.

The two enormous problems of personnel and financial resources have been discussed previously. It seems at least conceivable, however, that these crises (and they are that) also offer certain opportunities in Catholic education. Because traditional decision making structures proved inadequate to deal with these problems, the board movement developed. There has been an evolution in attitudes toward the presence of laymen in Catholic elementary and secondary schools—from the stage of viewing with alarm, through resignation, to appreciation of the distinctive and immensely important contribution of the lay teacher. The need for more money for education has caused enlightened dioceses and parishes to inform parishioners and the general community about the state of their finances. The necessity of raising funds from sources outside the Catholic community has forced Catholic educators to think more clearly about their needs and objectives and to explain these to the community at large. The challenge of collective bargaining between teachers and school systems brings with it an opportunity to create models of participative decision making and rational dialogue that can help other school systems and the Church itself.

Finally, the often difficult problems arising from an increased need of contact between public and nonpublic education can prove a boon to both educational systems. There is, one hopes, room in an affluent, democratic society for more than one educational enterprise. The value of this de facto pluralism, however, will go largely unrealized unless the respective systems communicate and cooperate with one another. Such communication and cooperation received powerful impetus from recent state and federal legislation that brought public and nonpublic authorities together for planning purposes, often for the first time. The same process should be enormously and quickly expanded to include educational policy makers, so that all educational systems in the country can be enriched through the "cross fertilization" resulting from dialogue among policy makers.

WILL CATHOLIC SCHOOLS SURVIVE?

Although whether Catholic schools will survive is clearly secondary to the larger question of why they should exist, nevertheless the issue of survival is important.

Enrollments in Catholic elementary and secondary schools are declining. Strictly speaking, the absolute number of high school students has shown only slight loss, but in the period 1964-1967 the percentage of students in Catholic high schools relative to the increasing national and Catholic population diminished perceptively. In 1967-1968 there were 1.07 million Catholic high school students, about 7.5 per cent of the nation's total high school population.

Catholic elementary school statistics show a greater decline, with 1967-1968 enrollments at 4.13 million, down from a 1963-1964 high of 4.55 million, and reduced more than 200,000 from the previous school year. Pupils in Catholic elementary schools comprise about 14 per cent of the American elementary school population.

Although these figures do not show enormous variations, they do manifest a trend likely to continue for some years. Shortages of personnel and funds severely limit expansion of Catholic schools in almost every sector of the country. As an increasing number of dioceses enact policies limiting class size and expanding curricular offerings, fewer children can be taught in the same number of classrooms by the same number of instructors. While school construction becomes increasingly expensive, the number of religious teachers continues to decline, and salaries of both lay and religious teachers are increasing at a more rapid rate than those of public school teachers. Consolidation of Catholic schools is usually welcomed by educators for increased advantages in curricular offerings, staff utilization, and administrative efficiency. But, typically, the merging of several schools results in an inability or unwillingness of some pupils to transfer to the consolidated school. Thus enrollments in these tend to be lower than the previous total for individual schools.

Despite these indicators it seems quite safe to predict that Catholic schools will indeed continue in this country. The reason is simple: a demand exists, and means are at hand to respond to that demand. If resources for continuing Catholic schools are not available to the extent desired, still those at hand are by no means negligible.

There seems even less reason to doubt the continuing demand for Catholic schools. Recent mandates by diocesan and parish boards to reduce staff-pupil ratios are unquestionably overdue. But pressures to increase enrollments in spite of staff limitations come primarily from parents. It is probably true that school policy makers and professional administrators should have resisted these pressures in the past more firmly for the sake of both pupils and teachers. It is quite clear, however, that parents regarded the values in Catholic schools as so compelling that they were willing to tolerate the disadvantages of large classes—and pay the tuition— in order to enroll their children in these schools.

UNIQUENESS OF CATHOLIC SCHOOLS

What qualities do these and several million other parents see in Catholic schools—that prompt them to bear the extra financial burdens? Or, to put the question another way, what is the unique contribution of the Catholic school?

Some Catholic parents, on being asked this question, offer reasons that are ill-founded, in philosophy or fact. Any school that can be selective in its admission and retention policies can choose its student body on the basis of religion, race, intelligence, or socioeconomic status, to mention some criteria. Undoubtedly some parents use nonpublic schools as preserves to keep their children from contact with children of different races, religions, or socioeconomic status. Parents also occasionally ascribe to the school powers and abilities it does not, in fact, possess.

Yet the demand for good Catholic schools at all levels will continue because these schools do offer students certain educational values prized by many Catholic parents. The need for a good "secular" education that prepares the student to live competently in the world around him is a requirement no parent can ignore for his child. The admittedly modest amount of evidence from national surveys shows that Catholic schools generally do a superior job of preparing students for adulthood.

A second school influence valued by parents is a good moral environment. This rather vague quality is measured especially by the general level of observed behavior of a school's student body and by the example and counsel given by the school staff. Again, this quality seems present at a relatively satisfactory level in most Catholic schools.

Both of these attributes, however, can be and frequently are found in public schools. Two additional influences desired by many parents for their children are customarily found only in religiously-oriented schools. These are (1) religious instruction and indoctrination and (2) religious activities. It is rare for public schools in this country to attempt instruction about religion below the college level, and it is clearly unconstitutional for them to attempt religious indoctrination or to sponsor religious activities. The ability to inculcate parent-approved values through formal periods of religious instruction and the relating of religious doctrine and values to "secular" subjects is one unique feature of the religious school. Religious activities such as daily prayer, in addition, help students translate this learning into desirable convictions and habits.

Teachers in most Catholic schools have substantial advantages in establishing rapport with their students, since they usually share with them a common religious orientation and can teach and counsel within this accepted system of beliefs and values. Furthermore, since attendance at Catholic schools is a matter of choice, usually involving considerable financial sacrifice, parental support of the Catholic school's procedures is normally quite high.

There seems little doubt that Catholic schools that offer an instructional program and a moral environment at least equal to that of local public schools, plus formal religious instruction and training, will continue to enjoy a "sellers' market." To be sure, demand alone does not guarantee the continuance of a school system beset by severe financial and personnel shortages. But the continuing appeal of schools uniquely able to perform certain much-desired educational tasks suggests a strongly affirmative reply to the question, "Should Catholic schools survive?"

X

Materials for Further Reading and Reference

Abbott, Walter M., S.J., *The Documents of Vatican II*, Guild Press, New York, 1966, 794 pp.

The Board of Parish Education, *Handbook for Local Boards of Christian Education*, The Lutheran Church-Missouri Synod, St. Louis, 32 pp.

Boffa, Conrad, *Canonical Provision for Catholic Schools*, The Catholic University of America Press, Washington, 1939, 211 pp.

Brouwer, John; Vander Ark, John A.; and Vander Ark, Mark, *Board Members Handbook*, Series 100, National Union of Christian Schools, Grand Rapids, 1961.

Brubacher, John W., *An Analysis of the Decision-Making Process of School Boards*, Doctoral Dissertation, University of Michigan, Ann Arbor, 1963, 225 pp.

Callahan, Raymond E., *Education and the Cult of Efficiency*, University of Chicago Press, Chicago, 1962, 273 pp.

Campbell, Roald F.; Cunningham, Luvern L.; and McPhee, Roderick E., *The Organization and Control of American Schools*, Charles E. Merrill Books, Columbus, Ohio, 1965, 553 pp.

Carter, Richard F., and others, *Communities and Their Schools*, Institute for Communication Research,

Stanford University, Stanford, Calif., 1960, 228 pp.

Carter, Richard F., *Voters and Their Schools,* Institute for Communication Research, Stanford University, Stanford, Calif., 1960, 311 pp.

Catholic Education Today and Tomorrow, edited by Michael P. Sheridan, S.J., and Russell Shaw, National Catholic Educational Association, Washington, 1968, 126 pp.

Concilii Plenarii Baltimorensis III Acta et Decreta, John Murphy Co., Baltimore, 1886, 2 vols.

D'Amour, O'Neil C., "Structural Change in Catholic Schools," *Catholic School Journal,* June, 1966, pp. 27-29.

Davies, Daniel R., and Brickell, Henry M., "The Board and the Curriculum," *School Board Policies,* Croft Educational Services, New London, Conn., March, 1963.

Deneen, James R., *Status of System-Wide School Boards in Catholic Dioceses in the United States,* Doctoral Dissertation, Indiana University, Bloomington, 1968, 123 pp.

DeWalt, Homer C., *An Analysis of the Status and the Functions of the Diocesan School Superintendency in the United States,* Doctoral Dissertation, University of Minnesota, Minneapolis, 1965, 327 pp.

Goldhammer, Keith, *The School Board,* The Center for Applied Research in Education, Inc., New York, 1964, 114 pp.

Greeley, Andrew M., and Rossi, Peter H., *The Education of Catholic Americans,* Aldine Publishing Co., Chicago, 1966.

Handbook for Committee Members of Friends Schools, Philadelphia Yearly Meeting of the Religious Society of Friends, Philadelphia, 1968.

McCoy, Raymond, *American School Administration, Catholic and Public,* McGraw-Hill, New York, 1961.

Management of Learning, New Dimensions in Higher Education, No. 5, U.S. Department of Health, Education and Welfare, Office of Education, U.S. Government Printing Office, Washington, 1960.

March, James G., and Simon, Herbert A., *Organizations,* John

Wiley and Sons, Inc., New York, 1958.

Moellet, Gerald H., "Teaching Perceptions of Administrative Behavior," Study jointly reported by Washington University, St. Louis, and the U.S. Office of Education, 1962.

Murdick, Olin J., *The Parish School Board*, N.C.E.A. Papers, The Association, Dayton, Ohio, 1967, 31 pp.

The National Catholic Educational Association, "Current Status of Diocesan School Boards," The Association, Washington, April, 1966, 2 pp.

National Conference of Catholic Bishops, *Statement on National Race Crisis*, The Conference, Washington, 1968, 7 pp.

Neuwien, Reginald, editor, *Catholic Schools in Action*, University of Notre Dame Press, Notre Dame, Ind., 1966.

New Directions in Catholic Education, A special issue of *Marriage* Magazine, Vol. 50, No. 1, January, 1968, 80 pp.

Parkman, Francis, and Springer, E. Laurence, *The Independent School Trustee*, National Association of Independent Schools, Boston, 1964, 68 pp.

Seidl, Anthony E., *Focus on Change—Management of Resources in Catholic Schools*, Joseph F. Wagner, Inc., New York, 1968, 218 pp.

Shaw, Russell, "The Pastor Has One Vote," *Ave Maria*, Vol. 105, No. 6, February 11, 1967, pp. 13-15.

Stapley, Maurice E., *School Board Studies*, Midwest Administration Center, University of Chicago Press, Chicago, 1957, 56 pp.

Voice of the Community: The Board Movement in Catholic Education, The Superintendents' Committee on Policy and Administration, National Catholic Educational Association, Dayton, Ohio, 1967, 47 pp.

63